POLITICS AND TELEVISION

Kurt Lang was formerly Research Sociologist for the Canadian Broadcasting Corporation and is now Professor of Sociology at the State University of New York at Stony Brook. His wife, Gladys Engel Lang, formerly Assistant Director of the Center for Urban Education in New York City, has taught sociology at Washington University and Carleton University (Ottawa), and is now in communications research and teaching at Columbia University. The Langs are co-winners of the Edward L. Bernays Award of the American Sociological Association for Research on the Effects of Television on American Life. They are also the authors of *Collective Dynamics*.

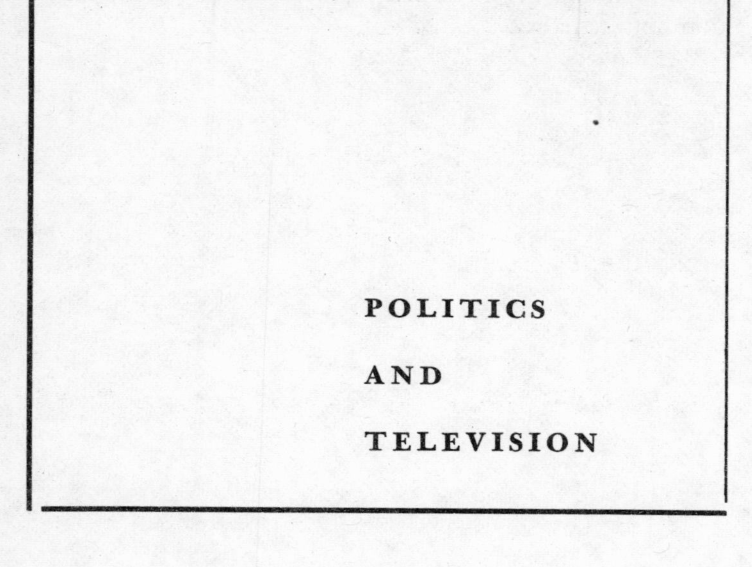

POLITICS AND TELEVISION

Kurt Lang and Gladys Engel Lang

QUADRANGLE BOOKS
Chicago

In memory of H. BERNHARD MOSBERG of the British Broadcasting System, a tireless monitor of radio broadcasts, who knew well the distinction between electronic communication and actuality

 For information,
address: Quadrangle Books, Inc., 12 East Delaware Place,
Chicago 60611.

Second Printing and first Quadrangle Paperback edition
published 1970.

Manufactured in the United States of America.

Library of Congress Catalog Card Number: 68-13460

PREFACE

As the first edition of this book went to press, the election campaign of 1968 was upon us, and—before the year was out—we had once again chosen a President. What part did television play in that choice? The question—especially the effects of the televising of the riotous Democratic convention—will be debated for years, as it has been after every election since television became a major medium of political communication in 1952.

Whatever the influence of television on the 1968 election, it will be said that it is hard to pinpoint and long in the making. It involves events preceding the campaign and is intertwined with a myriad of political factors that help to shape the images of candidates and parties and to define the issues of the campaign. Television is obviously only one among the news media—newspapers, magazines, radio, and so forth—that supply their audiences with a continuous flow of politically relevant information. Still, more and more, the events "seen" on television turn out to be most significant politically.

In this book we look at the ways in which television, through its presentation of events, shapes public images of political life and personalities. Our generalizations are products of sociological studies, each of some televised political event. In these studies we made use of social science techniques, like content analysis, surveys, and controlled observation, designed to get at viewer responses to events as they were happening—or just as soon after the telecasts as possible. Based on these findings about immediate responses to particular televised events, we have drawn some inferences—perhaps educated "guesses"—about the cumulative and long-range impact of television, about its past and potential effects.

If there is one main conclusion, it is that communication systems are human systems, no matter how powerful the means of visual and audio communication. Contrary to the McLuhanites, the medium is *not* the message. Television has no inherent capacity to convey "actuality" or the "truth." If the world now appears different from the way it appeared before television, this *does* have something to do with the way television is making it appear. But the way it appears depends on the way the men who employ the technology make use of it. They shape the content by their decisions, and these decisions often lead to effects other than those intended.

Though most chapters are based on articles previously published by the authors, they have been expanded, placed in historical context, and tied one to the other. Chapter II is a revision of an essay that won the Edward L. Bernays Award of the American Sociological Association in 1952, and appeared in abbreviated version in the *American Sociological Review,* February 1953. Chapters III to V are an outgrowth of a study of the 1952 nominating conventions, presented by Gladys Engel Lang for her Ph.D. dissertation ("Politics on Video," Department of Sociology, University of Chicago, 1954). Part of Chapter III previously appeared in the *Public Opinion Quarterly,* Fall 1955. Previous versions of Chapter V appeared in the *Public Opinion Quarterly,* Spring 1956, and in the *Journal of Broadcasting,* Winter 1956-1957.

The study of the televised debates, the topic of Chapter VI, was reported in the *Public Opinion Quarterly,* Summer 1961. Chapter VII presents the basic findings and conclusions of a study conducted under contract with the Columbia Broadcasting System. The report has been revised for publication and will appear in 1968 under the title *Voting and Nonvoting: Implications of Broadcasting Returns Before Polls Are Closed.*

Special acknowledgments are due Professor T. Shibutani for his help with the MacArthur Day study; to Dr. Donald Horton for his advice during the study of the 1952 political conventions; to Dr. Joseph T. Klapper for participation beyond the line of ordinary duty in the study of the 1964 election returns. Professor Bernard Rosenberg first suggested to Ivan R. Dee of Quadrangle Books that we put these essays together in book form.

KURT LANG

GLADYS ENGEL LANG

Stony Brook, New York
October 1969

CONTENTS

POLITICS AND TELEVISION

I

THE TELEVISION IMAGE

With the advent of film and radio, mass communications became a distinct area of sociological inquiry. Sociologists had long been concerned with the ways in which a reasonable consensus of opinion, necessary to the functioning of a pluralistic society, could be maintained or achieved. Now, the apparent ease with which images and ideas could be rapidly disseminated to a widely dispersed mass audience both interested and frightened them. Should control over the content of mass communication fall into the hands of a few persons, there were, it seemed, only vague limits to their power to mobilize mass sentiment in any direction, whether for good or for evil. That these media had an impact on political life, that they played an important part in the shaping of political imagery, and that they would bring about changes in political institutions was pretty much taken for granted. Students of mass media sought to pinpoint these effects, documenting in particular in what manner and under what conditions they occurred.

This is not, however, the way we tend to look at mass communication today. A sharp reorientation has taken place. By the time television arrived on the scene as the mass medium *par excellence,* sometime in the early 1950's, most research specialists had begun to play down the persuasive power once attributed to the mass media.

First of all, political events had a way of confounding commonsense assumptions about the ability of the mass media to engineer consent. Al Smith, governor of New York and Democratic candidate for President in 1928, had been the first political personality to star on radio; yet hadn't he suffered a stunning defeat? Subsequently, both Franklin D. Roosevelt and Harry S. Truman were able to win despite the overwhelming opposition of the press. Was this because of the good use they made of radio to counter newspaper influence? A systematic study of presidential campaigns in the United States indicated that a candidate's support by a majority of newspapers had not as a rule spelled the difference between victory and defeat.[1] By the same token, Eisenhower's 1952 victory in the first presidential campaign with nationwide television coverage was a personal triumph and hardly a simple consequence of the new medium. An analysis of public opinion polls taken in 1947 and 1948 showed that the general's popularity, including the wish to see him President, had clearly antedated the coming of television.[2]

If Eisenhower apparently won the 1952 election before the campaign even began, didn't the opportunity to display the famous personality on television contribute to his margin of victory? Again the evidence was essentially negative. Comparing persons who in following the campaign relied most heavily on television with those who relied more on some other mass medium (newspapers, radio, or news magazines) showed that television fans were, if anything, slightly more Democratic in their leanings. The difference was minor and probably not attributable to the use of television.[3] Another study compared voter turnout and the two-party distribution of the presidential vote in Iowa counties covered by television with other Iowa counties not yet within re-

1. Frank Luther Mott, "Newspapers in Presidential Campaigns," *Public Opinion Quarterly,* VIII (1944), 348–67.

2. Herbert Hyman and Paul B. Sheatsley, "The Political Appeal of President Eisenhower," *Public Opinion Quarterly,* XVII (Winter, 1953–54), 443–60.

3. Angus Campbell, Gerald Gurin, and Warren E. Miller, "Television and the Election," *Scientific American,* CLXXXVIII (1953), 46–48.

ceiving range of the signal. There was no significant difference in electoral behavior.[4]

Every time a new medium appears on the scene, we seem to expect revolutionary changes. The optimists stress its potential for education, the pessimists the possibility of abuse. For every expectation, so it appears, there is an equal and opposite expectation. Exorbitant claims are balanced by dire predictions, but most commentators agree that things will never be the same again.

One need only recall earlier moments from the history of communications. The era of religious conflict ushered in by the translation of the Bible into the vernacular coincided with the spread of cheap and efficient methods of printing that made it possible to put a copy into the hands of every literate believer. No one could be quite sure what would happen if each man were to become his own judge of the Word. Toward the end of the eighteenth century in Britain, where the freedom of the printed word had long been proclaimed (though not always honored in practice), the opening to the press of parliamentary debates posed a similar problem about the effects of so much "informed" opinion. And so it was later on with the coming of the mass-circulation newspaper. Hailed as an instrument of education, it also suffered the charge that its circulation stunts played on

4. Herbert A. Simon and F. Stern, "The Effect of Television upon Voting Behavior in Iowa in the 1952 Presidential Election," *American Political Science Review*, XLIX (June, 1955), 470–78.

the lowest passions. The excesses of "yellow" journalism, the propaganda of atrocity in World War I, and the "ballyhoo" of the 1920's readily come to mind. Radio raised new hopes, but Hitler's extensive use of it as his preferred medium of propaganda also left an indelible memory. Hence, the arrival of television, though it coincided with a period of relative political quiescence, was coupled with the imagined rise of Madison Avenue as the seat of dominant power. Although the medium could be used for elevating the political consciousness of the public, many feared that politics would now be marketed much like toothpaste. Anything could be sold with the appropriate formula.

Social scientists specializing in mass communications research were more cautious. Research efforts, begun before World War II and reaching fruition in the postwar decade, pointed to the limits of mass media influence—and the effects of television were subject to the same limits. Studies showed that individual responses to particular messages transmitted by the mass media were shaped by personal dispositions and competing influences. Mass communication effects, as Joseph Klapper summarized these findings, always occur together with a whole host of mediating factors, which all together help reinforce pre-existing tendencies.[5] Changes in attitudes, beliefs, and behavior directly traceable to the mass media are the exception rather than the rule. This

5. Joseph T. Klapper, *The Effects of Mass Communication*, Glencoe, Ill., Free Press, 1960.

is because exposure is highly self-selective; people pay attention primarily to content that already interests them and that is congenial to their point of view.

This selective exposure is made possible by the pluralistic structure of the mass media in the United States. But even when people do expose themselves to contrary or unfamiliar points of view, their interpretations of a message are often different from those intended by the sender. A final limitation on media influence resides in the situation in which the response takes place. Whether or not people follow through on the intent of a message depends at least in part on available opportunities for doing so and on whether this response is condoned or proscribed by their immediate associates.

The upshot of all these findings was to temper exuberance about the educational potential of the mass media and, at the same time, to calm fears about the deleterious effects of propaganda. At least it could be stated with some confidence that these hopes and fears received little support from research. Yet there was still some unease, even among those who themselves were documenting the minimal effects attributable to the mass media. Like others, they continued to talk privately —and sometimes to act publicly—as if they still somehow believed in the potency of the media. In 1952, the faculties of the great universities, including some of those whose work was constantly cited to illustrate the relative unimportance of mass media influences, waged a battle of newspaper ads in support of Stevenson or Eisenhower. Lacking final answers, they clung to the belief that the mass media were perhaps more influential than they would otherwise wish. Outcries against television performances—like the famous 1952 speech in which Vice President Nixon invoked the name of his dog "Checkers," or Senator McCarthy's behavior during the so-called Army-McCarthy hearings in 1954—as well as the enduring and enthusiastic acceptance accorded to George Orwell's *1984* supported vividly the researchers' suspicions that perhaps research did not tell them what common sense revealed was there to be told.

This uneasiness about the conclusions of most research was voiced by the late Eugene Burdick, a political scientist, when he was assembling a collection of essays on voting behavior. In 1956, he wrote to the authors:

> The volume [I am preparing] will contain chapters on almost all of the recent voting studies including the Berelson-Lazarsfeld-McPhee volume, the Michigan Survey Research Center work and some British material. One thing that stands out in all of this, however, is the relative insignificance of the mass media in influencing the voter's decision. . . . It occurs to me that much of the alleged impotence of the mass media may be due to the fact that the studies were not specifically set up to catch this aspect of voting. I judge (from what I have heard) that you think the mass media may have a much more decisive impact than most scholars believe.

In our answer we tried to set down our reasons for not sharing the conclusion many researchers had adopted at that time. Failure to pinpoint the effects of the media, we wrote, lay:

in the researcher's expectation that there must be some particular and, moreover, short-run change traceable to a particular exposure (or exposures) or to some particular medium. In short, we tend to be disappointed when the mass media "reinforce" rather than "convert" or when television, for example, appears to have no immediately discernible impact on those directly exposed.

It follows further from this expectation that observations are usually conducted when some particular response, e.g., casting a vote, is demanded. Studies on the effects of the mass media on voting are conducted during campaigns, when people know that they are being propagandized, whereas certain media materials not ostensibly part of the campaign may constitute the crucial test. We also object to the new trend which sees personal influence as dominant everywhere. A recent book[6] is supposed to show that "personal influence" [the influence of one person on another] is more important than "mass influence" [the influence of the mass media on the person]. This focus on the ubiquity of personal influence overlooks the fact that any lasting impact the mass media do have occurs within a context of relations and pressures that exist independent of them. The "opinion leader" [the person who influences others] often acts only as a transmitter of news or information, usually of something that has already become the focus of some interest, however vaguely defined, because it has been carried by the mass media. While this transmittal function of "opinion leaders" is usually recognized in a footnote, the fact that the influencee cites the influencer [opinion leader] as the source of his information is inter-

6. Elihu Katz and Paul Lazarsfeld, *Personal Influence*, Glencoe, Ill., Free Press, 1955.

> preted as proof for the relative importance of personal influence.
>
> In other words, we feel that the mass media structure issues and personalities. They do this gradually and over a period of time, and thus this impact seems less spectacular than the shift or crystallization of a particular vote decision. We cannot help but believe that, indirectly, by creating a political climate, a sense of urgency, an image of parties and candidates, etc., they do influence votes.

These views were not entirely a matter of wishful thinking or unwarranted suspicion. They were in part based on what our own research effort had been demonstrating. In that research we were concerned less with the specific responses of individuals than with the way political events were being structured and influenced by the presence of a new medium. The issue was not, to paraphrase John Dewey, so much that communications affect the political community but that society exists only in communication.[7] Television might provide a new kind of social experience with implications for the political process. The nature of this experience had to be studied.

The Age of Television

The era of radio seems to have passed so quickly that its impact on political life had hardly been considered

7. See *The Public and Its Problems.*

when the "new age of television" arrived.[8] Most of us remember the major milestones of television "firsts," in which the dramatic potential of that medium for disseminating public events was initially revealed. The first generation of children who cannot remember life without a television set were just coming of voting age in 1968. Politics without video is inconceivable to them.

The discussions of mass media experts in the early 1950's, when nationwide coverage first became a reality, centered on the "front-row seat" that television gave every viewer. Enthusiasts believed that television, because it enlarged the viewer's social world beyond belief, enabled him to become intimately acquainted with persons and places to which he would never, without television, have access. It transformed the mass society into a mass neighborhood. Television's personalities entered the daily lives of people and involved them in interactions that have been called "para-social." [9] The characters in TV serials and hosts of other programs became significant social personalities with whom interactions were sustained. Public participation, via video, in the political life of the country would have a similar para-social character.

What were the major events that first aroused our interest in political television? In 1950, a Senate subcommittee's investigations into organized crime were

8. A term first publicized by Leo Bogart in his book by that title (New York, Frederick Ungar, 1956).

9. Donald Horton and R. Richard Wohl, "Mass Communications and Para-Social Interaction," *Psychiatry*, XIX (August, 1956), 215–29.

televised. Witness after witness from gangland was paraded before the TV camera and subjected to questioning by Senator Kefauver and his chief counsel, Rudolph Halley. The committee's investigations brought to the national consciousness the prevalence of crime. One investigation of the public response to the hearings indicated a high degree of emotional arousal and indignation, but when it came to doing something to remedy the situation, this study indicated that only a small minority of persons were sufficiently motivated to take even modest political action, such as writing to their congressman.[10] Could it therefore be said that the presence of the television cameras had no effect? Crime and corruption became one of the major issues in the 1952 elections, and Kefauver, thanks to television, emerged as its chief opponent to become a leading contender for the Democratic nomination and, in 1956, ultimately to be nominated for Vice President. His chief counsel was elected president of the New York City Council, winning against the Democratic machine.

In 1951, television's role in another event made us question the allegedly automatic reportorial accuracy of video reporting. On April 11, in the midst of the Korean War, President Harry S. Truman's summary dismissal of General Douglas MacArthur, a World War II hero and commander-in-chief of the American forces

10. G. D. Wiebe, "Responses to the Televised Kefauver Hearings: Some Social Psychological Implications," *Public Opinion Quarterly*, XVI (Summer, 1952), 179–200.

engaged in battle, stirred up a national furor. The White House communiqué relieving MacArthur of all his commands clearly stated the reason for dismissal: the general, through his public statements, had repeatedly invaded the field of policy-making, the prerogative of the President. The statement concluded with deep regret that "General MacArthur is unable to give his wholehearted support to the policies of the United States government and of the United Nations in matters pertaining to his official duties." In other words, he was dismissed for insubordination and not for technical incompetence.

MacArthur's departure from Japan, a week after his dismissal, and his homeward journey after fourteen years of continuous service abroad were more like a triumphal march than a voluntary acceptance of the President's supreme authority. A reporter and a historian, in describing the mood of the country, said it was doubtful "if there has ever been in this country so violent and spontaneous a discharge of political passion as that provoked by the President's dismissal of the General and by the General's dramatic return from his voluntary patriotic exile."[11]

All this had little to do with television. But from the moment MacArthur reached the continental United States, television cameras accompanied him on every public appearance from his first landing in San Fran-

11. Richard H. Rovere and Arthur M. Schlesinger, Jr., *The General and the President,* New York, Farrar, Straus, 1951, p. 5.

cisco, where he received a hero's welcome, to his stops in other cities, large and small. The press reports, including television newsreels, of his reception gave an impression of mass hysteria and an active outpouring of political outrage. The authors were then residing in Chicago, and MacArthur Day as celebrated there seemed to offer a unique opportunity for a systematic study of crowd behavior and of the role of the media of mass communication, particularly television, in this kind of event.

Our main goal was stymied. The air of curiosity and casualness exhibited by most members of the crowd was a surprise to every observer reporting from the scene. But those watching the televised welcome saw pretty much what they had expected to see. What intrigued us was: why should "reality" as experienced over television have diverged so much from the "reality" of personal participation in the event? Those who participated in the study could no longer believe that reportorial accuracy was intrinsic in the technical capabilities of television.

The MacArthur Day study has sometimes been cited as proof of *deliberate* distortion by news media.[12] This interpretation of our findings misses the point. In Chapter II we offer a more detailed account of these findings and an explanation of the reasons for "unwitting" bias. Intensive study of the 1952 political conventions (the

12. See, for example, remarks made during the Corning Conference included in Eugene Staley, *Creating an Industrial Civilization,* New York, Harper, 1952, p. 82.

subject of Chapters III and IV) provides further insight into the processes that lead to distorted impressions of televised events.

With our interest once aroused by MacArthur Day, it was natural that we should turn our attention to the presidential campaign as it was shaping up for 1952. Not only were both political conventions to receive national political coverage for the first time, but this promised to be the first campaign in which both parties would make a major investment in television.

The 1952 Republican convention turned into a two-way contest, with Eisenhower gaining a narrow victory over Senator Taft. The convention "proved," in the words of ABC commentator Elmer Davis, that "it was no longer possible to commit grand larceny in broad daylight"—in other words, in front of the glaring eyes of the TV cameras. "Larceny" referred to the dispute over the seating of contested delegations from three Southern states; the resolution of the dispute turned out to be crucial for the outcome of the nomination, because the successful challenge of credentials enabled Eisenhower to get enough additional delegates to be assured the nomination. But whether and how television affected the public response and, through it, the decision of the convention are quite other questions.

A more deliberate effort to use television to solicit a public reaction occurred during the campaign and aroused our curiosity about the "television personality." It made us wonder in particular about the supposedly terrifying capacity of the television camera to reveal the truth and to expose disingenuousness of every sort. Thus, Adlai Stevenson, who clearly could not resist a joke, especially on himself, insisted after the 1952 election that he had "clearly won the bosom-beating and public-stripping contest of last fall." The issue he raised is a serious one, however. It concerned the successful defense by Richard M. Nixon, in front of the television cameras, of the $18,235 expense fund donated by seventy-six of his California supporters.

It may be recalled that in 1952 "the mess in Washington" was one of the major themes of the Republican campaign. Yet, in the middle of the campaign some enterprising reporters unearthed a story about the Nixon expense fund. As this news slowly snowballed, pressure mounted for Nixon to withdraw from the "anti-corruption" ticket. Eisenhower was reported to be collecting facts and pondering a decision. When it was announced that Nixon would offer a full explanation in a half-hour television broadcast, this announcement immediately became front-page news, and the interest aroused gave Nixon the largest television audience ever for any campaign speech.[13]

Nixon's half-hour program was produced by an advertising agency. For the first fifteen minutes he sat behind a desk and spoke directly to the audience. In

13. The speech was carried by 194 stations of the Columbia Broadcasting System and by the sixty-two-station hook-up of the National Broadcasting Company's television network. NBC estimated, without making an audience count, that the program was "possibly" seen by 25 million people. Mutual Broadcasting estimated that 90 per cent of the nation's 45 million radio homes were tuned in.

simple and measured words, he told about his personal ordeal in having his honesty and integrity questioned when he had a big mortgage on his house and his wife was wearing a cloth coat, not a fur coat. During the second fifteen minutes he moved out from behind his desk and stood talking to the audience; the camera, at appropriate moments, revealed Mrs. Nixon looking at her husband as he addressed the television audience. The broadcast concluded with an unprecedented appeal to the public to wire and write the Republican National Committee, as the chief authority over his campaign, whether or not he should be dropped from the ticket.

The press reported an avalanche of letters, telegrams, and telephone calls overwhelmingly in favor of Nixon. The national committee said its mail ran 350 to 1 to keep him on the ticket. Senator Nixon flew to Wheeling, West Virginia, where Eisenhower publicly embraced him with the words, "You're my boy." As a result of this speech, Nixon had not only turned to his (and his party's) advantage what could have been a disaster for both, but he had also gained in stature. He had become a public figure in his own right, not just another running mate. To many he was a hero, and his speech stimulated new interest in the flagging campaign. It also generated public accountings of finances and explanations of income taxes paid by the three other national candidates.

Regardless of whether the Nixon speech won the Republicans additional votes, its impact on images could not be denied. The Oxford Associates reported that among their panel of television viewers in Ohio, Democratic voters were more ready to concede that Nixon acted ethically in using this fund than were Republican voters ready to grant that Governor Stevenson had done no moral wrong in soliciting funds from anonymous donors to supplement the low salaries of Illinois public servants and thus lure competent men into his administration.[14]

Many commentators have pondered the symbolism Nixon used to make his appeal, but few have dealt directly with some of the more basic issues involved in this usage of television. Indicative of the former is the comment by Gilbert Seldes, who some months later asked, "Did the camera panning over to Mrs. Nixon add the image of 'Whistler's Mother' (the pose was similar) to the verbal stimulus of Nixon's emphasis on 'Pat' and March 17 as her birthday?" Nixon talked of a little cocker spaniel, which he had accepted as a gift for his children. He made use of other market-tested symbols to convey his personal honor and love for his country. To this he tacked on a routine campaign speech, in which he attacked his opponents and gave effusive praise to General Eisenhower who was listening and said to be

14. Miami University, Department of Marketing, *The Influence of Television on the Election of 1952,* Oxford, Ohio, Oxford Research Associates. December, 1954, p. 177.

trying to reach a decision on Nixon's place on the ticket.[15]

Nixon himself, after resuming the campaign trail, marveled how a person from the humble background that was his could run for high office and when attacked could go on television and radio, where all he had to do was tell the truth. Thus an issue of political morality was transformed into one of personal honesty. Press comment about how the "man in the street" reacted revealed this only too clearly:

> The people who own dogs like I do are for Nixon. That story about the dog for his children made me love him.
>
> Nixon was so utterly sincere that no one could doubt his honesty.

Or a deviant reaction:

> I think he told a lot of lies. He's just too young to be in there.

While there was much criticism of Nixon's unscrupulous use of theatrics, his "soap-opera" appeal, the low level of intelligence at which he had pitched his defense, and the use of show business methods in politics, no one could deny that his political technique had been effective. But what about "appealing" one's case to the

15. Some of Seldes' comments are contained in *The Public Arts,* New York, Simon and Schuster, 1956.

great American "jury," when there were no rules of evidence? Was television's capacity for revealing the "truth" so inescapable that no one would mistake the rehearsed speech for spontaneity? And what kind of precedent did it set for standards of political debate in the future?

In transferring true and tried propaganda techniques to a medium whose effects were so immediate, there might result what Walter Lippmann called "mob law by modern electronics." Many of us shared his misgivings over the new partnership between television and public life and, like him, were disturbed while watching Nixon's fight for his political life. Wrote Lippmann:

> The charges against Senator Nixon were so serious that for five days General Eisenhower reserved his own judgment on whether to clear him or condemn him. Why? Because the evidence, the law, and the moral principles at issue are none of them simple or obvious. . . . They have to do with matters which can then be decided only by some sort of judicial process. How, then, can a television audience be asked or allowed to judge the matter before General Eisenhower finished his inquiry and reached his conclusion? . . . What the television audience should have been given was not Senator Nixon's personal defense. That should have been made first before General Eisenhower. What the television audience should have been given was General Eisenhower's decision, backed by a full and objective account of the facts and of the points of law and of morals which are involved.

The whole question of the television personality in

politics, which is the subject of Chapter V, was raised by still other events. The televised Army-McCarthy hearings, in which the Wisconsin senator attempted to bulldoze with reckless charges several members of the defense establishment, held the country's attention in 1954. These hearings certainly coincided with the turn in the senator's fortunes, and television is often cited as a major cause of McCarthy's downfall and his censure by the Senate. In front of the pitiless TV cameras, it was alleged, McCarthy revealed himself to the public not as a patriot but as the demagogue he actually was.

We know of no evidence to support this simple an explanation. McCarthy's standing in the polls began to slip only after the Senate moved to take action against him. Hence, whatever role television played in the destruction of the myth of McCarthy's invincibility was certainly something different than a mass reaction to his antics before the cameras. Had not the Nixon episode shown that important issues could be sidestepped without this redounding to the detriment of the candidate? After the hearings, powerful political forces in the Senate and on Capitol Hill were finally stirred to action. McCarthy's public performance was among the actions they used to discredit him. The Nixon speech, by contrast, was not only a smoother performance, but as campaign oratory it was less open to challenge.

The Army-McCarthy hearings also marked the first time that one of McCarthy's charges met an immediate challenge from an opposing counsel. This happened during an interchange with lawyer Joseph Welch that had all markings of a courtroom drama. The "instant reply" was subsequently built into the televised debates of 1960, in which Richard M. Nixon was paired against John F. Kennedy. Our study of this confrontation, reported in Chapter VI, shows again how responses to a television personality are determined by political convictions. If this is so, we can infer that the dramatic impact of Nixon's "Checkers" speech on millions of viewers—we made no study of our own of this incident—was less a product of what he said than a reflection of Eisenhower's great appeal to voters. Many persons, Republicans and Democrats alike, did not want to see the general embarrassed politically and hence were ready to exonerate Nixon as long as he offered them a rationale for doing so.

A final issue concerns the implications of television, as a medium of political communication, for the functioning of the institutions of government. The televised presidential press conference has become an established institution. It appears that, as a result, the interchange between the President and reporters may be less free than it was before. On the other hand, pressure for televised debates between contenders for major political offices is building. There are demands for modifications of the "equal time" provision to enable the networks to accommodate these debates without undue loss of revenue.

The latest of the innovations in communications technology concerns the quick dissemination of presidential election returns to the public while polling in some areas of the country is still in progress. This is the subject of Chapter VII. Again our interest lies mainly in how political perceptions concerning the electoral process may be influenced by the new techniques of mass communication, all of which together make possible a freer and more unimpeded flow of political information to the public.

Television and Public Events

The studies in this book are of events that have made television history. The excitement over the events themselves is gone. We can recapture for ourselves only with some difficulty our own sense of involvement in the events at the time the studies were in process. Nevertheless, we believe that they touch on rather general issues and are, to that extent, not dated. A concern with images of politics, of politicians, and of political moods is the common theme that ties all of them together.

If these studies diverge in many respects from usual studies of perception, this is because we treat the viewer not solely as an observer who is the target of certain messages, but also as a participant in the events he observes over video. What is the nature of such participation in televised public events? Does it affect the viewer's imagery of the political process and, indirectly, his electoral behavior? Do politicians and political institutions accommodate themselves to this new form of political participation? What are the processes involved, and what long-term changes seem to result?

To characterize our interest in these events as sociological is to distinguish it from that of the journalist (or historian) who offers a meaningful account of what transpired during a particular event, as well as from that of other researchers whose primary concern is with documenting and measuring a particular effect as precisely as possible—What candidate was helped? Who won the debate? And so forth. Knowledge about how high audience ratings are achieved or how attitude change is maximized is important for the effective use of television to achieve specific goals. Yet these instrumental uses of television do not exhaust all aspects of the myriad relationships between television and politics. We naturally assume that every event has some kind of effect; our idea is to so conduct the study of any event that, once it is over, we can depict and analyze in some detail *whatever* effects turn up. This often takes us in new and sometimes unanticipated directions. Insights obtained from these attempts to assess and understand the impact of the events in question then become the starting points for entirely new lines of inquiry.

This is not to say, however, that this kind of inquiry is altogether without focus. Rather, we have been guided in a general way by several popular assumptions about the effects of television, effects which are assumed to be intrinsic to the medium and not usually subjected to direct scrutiny. These effects usually refer, in one way or another, to the intimacy, simultaneity, directness, and completeness of the view afforded by television.

(1) Many people have voiced the opinion that tele-

vision, because it affords a close-up view of personalities and events, creates a sense of familiarity with public figures, political activities, and distant places. This type of face-to-face contact is presumed to result in a sense of "intimacy" and personalization of politics.

(2) Again, by adding sight to sound, television is said to do more than combine a newsreel or movie with radio broadcasting. Where the telecast is live, visual simultaneity provides a dimension of experience that is like being transported to the scene. This unique characteristic of television results in the viewer's "being there" and allows him to participate directly in public affairs.

(3) A third consequence supposedly follows from this characteristic of the medium *per se:* because viewers can see "for themselves" and the camera "does not lie," a more authentic picture of public events than hitherto possible is disseminated. The public no longer must rely on a third party to report what goes on. They can formulate their own judgments without danger of being victims of others' biases or interpretations.

(4) As long as there is full coverage, the vantage point provided by television results in a picture of what is taking place that is fuller, richer, and more complete than that conveyed by other media. "Watching over TV" may not only be as good as "being there"; it may in fact be better.

No one study can possibly answer all the questions that these assumptions raise about the role of television in politics. But if some of the effects inferred from the technological capabilities of the medium are real, they may be less the direct result of technology than of the fact that people have come to *believe* that these effects exist. Accordingly, the assumptions that govern the "use" of television may be real in their consequences, because members of the audience, mass communicators, and the public figures who are the televised "objects" act "as if" certain qualities inhered in the coverage. This effect is constantly in mind throughout our studies.

II

MacARTHUR DAY IN CHICAGO

Since Admiral Dewey was "spontaneously" invited to a hero's welcome by cities throughout the United States, such receptions have become traditional. Through such ceremonies America pays tribute to its great heroes, its men of achievement. Promotion helps along the enthusiasm. Silas Bent documented, in his book on *Ballyhoo,*[1] how already in the 1920's some crusading newspapers

1. Silas Bent, *Ballyhoo: The Voice of the Press,* New York, Boni and Liveright, 1927.

had raised the mobilization of enthusiasm to the status of an art, how celebrities are induced to lend their names to receptions, and community organizations and local governments to cooperate. Once this has been done, the mass of spectators need only contribute their presence and vocal power, throw ticker tape, and snatch up insignia.

The homecoming of General Douglas MacArthur in 1951 offered a chance to revive a custom last practiced when other military leaders of World War II returned some six years before. In 1951, cities—big and small—were quick to ask the general to honor them with a visit. On April 16, Democratic Mayor Martin H. Kennelly extended Chicago's official invitation. It was in this same spirit that on the next day, following a plan by a WGN radio commentator, Chicagoans could hear whistles, firecrackers, and church bells—or so one read in the newspapers on April 18—exactly at the time the plane bearing MacArthur touched American soil in San Francisco.

Yet there were other overtones of MacArthur's triumphal return. In the two weeks between the general's dismissal and his reception in Chicago on April 26, the press featured stories indicating widespread public indignation. State legislatures passed resolutions of their trust in the general and their condemnation of the President's action. In Congress there were some unusually vitriolic attacks on Truman and his backers. For instance, a Republican senator applied the epithet "pygmies" to those who had tried to "bring down this tower of strength and deserving idol of the American people." Three senators actually came to blows during one of the more heated exchanges. Meanwhile, news reports from every section of the country told of effigies of Truman and Dean Acheson, his Secretary of State, hanging from trees. Tempers appeared to have been stretched to the breaking point in a divided country.

Developments were clearly moving toward some climax when, upon reaching Washington, General MacArthur made a memorable address to a joint meeting of both houses of Congress, at the close of which he promised that like an "old soldier" he would "fade away." The speech was reported to have had an electrifying effect on the nation. Few thought it a contradiction to this avowed self-effacement for MacArthur to go on to a triumphal homecoming in New York. Then, after nearly a week of relative obscurity, he emerged again to receive what Chicago promised would be an ear-splitting welcome, second to none.

MacArthur Day in Chicago included the following events, all of them televised: MacArthur's arrival and greeting at Midway Airport; a motorcade and parade through the city, with a stop at the Bataan-Corregidor Bridge to lay a wreath in honor of the war dead; the resumption of the parade through the heart of Chicago's business district; and an evening rally at Soldier Field, where the general gave a speech. Chicagoans could participate as spectators at any of these events. They could likewise view any or all of them on television. The number along the parade route together with those who viewed the event over TV must have added up to a sizable proportion of Chicago's population. It was a genuine public event.

The Study

The idea of systematically studying what was to happen on MacArthur Day came up in an advanced seminar on crowd behavior and social contagion that Dr. Tamotsu Shibutani was then conducting at the University of Chicago. The suggestion met with a spontaneously warm response. Because there were less than seventy-two hours between suggestion and event, we were in some haste to formulate hypotheses, design procedures, recruit fellow graduate students as volunteer observers, and make all the concrete preparations necessary to carry out an investigation of this sort.

The study was, by design, open-ended, an effort to "explore" rather than test specific propositions. Our aim was to get maximum coverage of the event. To this end we assigned volunteer observers so that no important spot in the general's itinerary, where crowds could be observed, was neglected. There were thirty-one observers so distributed that some were able to cover the day's events from more than one station. An observer could, for instance, witness the arrival at the airport and still arrive in Chicago's Loop in time to see the downtown parade. The resulting coverage thus was based on some forty-three perspectives.

Observers received instructions that they were both well trained and highly motivated to carry out. These called special attention to the need to discriminate in their reports between their own subjective feelings and what they were able to observe about others—who said and did what, how, where, and when.

In addition, two persons monitored the TV coverage, the audio portion of which was also recorded on tape. Because of our interest in television, observers on the scene were asked to take special note of anything indicating possible influences of television on the event, such as action directed toward the TV cameras or stag ing for the benefit of TV.

When we compared the various observers' reports, it became strongly evident that the MacArthur Day reported by persons on the scene was rather different from MacArthur Day as it appeared to the televiewer. This contrast between the two perspectives of MacArthur Day led us to inquire into possible causes and, from this basis, to assess the role television played in the presentation of public events and its significance in politics generally.

The Pattern of Expectations

As a rule, the mass media prepare the ground for the way an event is seen. MacArthur Day seemed to be no exception. Certainly the crowd which turned out for the motorcade and parade was far from a casual collection of individuals: its members *intended* to be witnesses to an "unusual" event. The pattern of expectations became apparent from two sources: the statements of spectators (recorded in observer reports) about what they expected to occur and the personal accounts of the thirty-one observers indicating what they themselves had expected, accounts they had written on the eve of MacArthur Day.

Both sets of data pointed to the same thing. Many of the spectators had *anticipated* "mobs" and "wild crowds." They had expected some disruption of transportation schedules. They had come downtown in search of adventure and excitement. When all overheard and solicited conversations were tabulated for the expectation they contained, one-third concerned such wild—perhaps threatening—scenes. Leaving aside another quarter of the remarks alluding to purely personal hopes (being able to see, photograph, wave to MacArthur), the second largest group of remarks emphasized the "spectacle." This table sums up what the *spectators* expected:

Expectation	%
Disorderly conduct and excitement, disruption of facilities (due to "crowd behavior," that is, an implicit *threat*)	37%
A chance to hail, photograph the hero (the *personal* anticipation)	27%
Extraordinary magnitude regarding showmanship and turnout	19%
Factual expectations (time of arrival, etc.)	7%
Display of political sentiment	2%
Other	8%
All expectations as evidenced by remarks	100%

Expectations of the *observers* differed slightly in emphasis but not in content from those of the spectators they observed. This difference can be accounted for, in part, by the observers' "unrepresentativeness" (they had a special interest in participating) and, in part, by the different conditions under which their expectations were elicited. Each of these volunteer observers filled out a personal data sheet before setting forth to observe. As a result of an unfortunate collapsing of several questions into one, the response did not always focus properly on what observers themselves "expected to see." Of those who clearly stated their personal anticipations, two-thirds expected excited and wildly enthusiastic crowds. But it is a safe guess, when we recall the discussion during the briefing session, that the number who expected such crowds was considerably higher. After all, as pointed out in Chapter I, the main incentive to volunteer was the opportunity to study crowd behavior at first hand.

To sum up: most people expected a wild spectacle in which large masses of onlookers would take an active part, and which contained an element of threat in view of the heightened emotions and the power of large numbers.

A more detailed examination of these same data shows that this pattern of expectations was shaped by the mass media. For it is in this way that the picture of the larger world comes to sophisticated as well as unsophisticated people. The observers were no exception to this dependence on what newspapers, newsreels, and television cameras told them; they were perhaps better able than others to describe the origin of such impressions. Thus, Observer 14 wrote:

> I had listened to the accounts of MacArthur's arrival in San Francisco, heard radio reports of his progress through the United States, and had heard the Washington speech as well as the radio accounts of his New York reception. . . . I had therefore expected the crowds to be much more vehement, contagious, and identified with MacArthur. I had expected to hear much political talk, especially anti-communist and against the Truman administration. These expectations were completely unfulfilled. I was amazed that not once did I hear Truman criticized, Acheson mentioned, or as much as an allusion to the communists. . . . I had expected roaring, excited mobs. Instead there were quiet, well-ordered, dignified people. . . . The air of curiosity and casualness surprised me. Most people seemed to look on the event as simply something that might be interesting to watch.

Here are some very similar notations by other observers:

> I had expected—after reading, and seeing newsreels of his reception in other cities—tremendous enthusiasm, larger crowds, and louder cheering. As it was, I could not quite figure out why people were there, unless it was to see how other people acted and in the expectation of seeing a magnificent spectacle, of the sort which had been promised by the newspapers.

> The wave of sentiment and excitement that passed through this group was surprisingly below what this observer had anticipated as a result of listening to the

> radio broadcast of his [MacArthur's] arrival in San Francisco and the parade in Washington, D.C. The feeling of participation in a genuinely excited crowd was almost absent. Certainly at no point were they carried away, nor did they experience or express strong sentiments, except in isolated, individual cases.

We wanted to observe the event in its natural context, so this meant forgoing the use of a formal or even an informal interview, in which people, especially those with television sets at home, could have been asked *why* they had forsaken the comforts of home viewing to take themselves or their families downtown. Because such standardized data are missing, the *why* cannot be fully answered. But this much could be ascertained: people expected to take part in an event, the full flavor of which was to be savored only by direct participation in it. Conversations recorded by observers provide ample evidence that spectators, like the observers themselves, inferred a mood, a feeling of enthusiasm, a throb of excitement. Though they had already *read* about it, *heard* about it, or even *seen* it for themselves (on TV news shows), they felt they could appreciate and share in it fully only by being present.

As they waited for the parade, many made comparisons between the advantages of "being there" and "seeing it over television." The conveniences and intimacy of the family circle were weighed against the opportunity of taking an active part. Said a father with two children:

> Sure, it's more fun than seeing it on TV. People are simply too lazy to take their kids out; no wonder there's communism.

An elderly woman answered an observer's conversational gambit that he "could have been watching from an office window":

> My gosh, how come you're out here! Of course, I could have been sitting home and seeing this much better on TV, but I decided I'd just like to be in a crowd today.

What brought people out? Why were they there? Observers, though instructed to report concrete behavior rather than general interpretations, did at intervals or at the end of the day generalize their impressions. All generalizations on the motivation of the crowd were either of two kinds: that crowds had turned out to see a great military figure and public hero "in the flesh," or—the logical supplement of the first—that they had turned out not so much "to see *him,* as I noticed, but to see the *spectacle.*"

No observer supported the official view, stressed by the mass media, that people had come to find vantage points from which to see the man and his family so as to welcome, cheer, and honor him. Yet among the concrete behavior these observers reported there were isolated incidents which would justify such an interpretation.

Actual incidents, behavior, and statements recorded

were even more revealing of why people had joined the crowd. Each was classified as lending support to one of the three above-mentioned generalizations as to why people were there—to see a celebrity whose arrival had been widely publicized, to find excitement and witness an unusual spectacle, and to pay homage as an act of hero worship. When tabulated, here were the results:

Interest in seeing MacArthur	48%
Passive interest in the spectacle	42%
Active hero worship	9%
(1% not classifiable)	

At first glance these figures seem to contradict the contention that people were mainly anticipating a spectacle, a great show of some sort. But, in the first place, interest in the spectacle did not preclude a secondary interest in seeing MacArthur—the spectacle did revolve around him, and in many ways these two interests were complementary. More important, when these observations are broken down according to the area in which they were observed, it is clear that the crowds in the Loop, the great bulk of the participant spectators who took part in MacArthur Day, thought of the occasion *primarily* as a spectacle. There in the Loop, in the heart of Chicago, 60 per cent of the observations supported the "spectacle hypothesis." Contrast this with percentages in other areas: Negro district, 40; Soldier Field, 23; Airport, 18; University of Chicago area, 0.

The Unfulfilled Expectation

This probe into motivation helps to confirm the pattern of expectations observed. To this evidence should be added those constantly overheard expressions—which increased as time spent waiting increased and the expected excitement failed to materialize—of disillusionment with particular vantage points. "We should have stayed home and watched it on TV" was the almost universal way in which such dissatisfaction was verbalized. Compared with the spectator's experience of extended boredom and sore feet, alleviated only by a brief glimpse of the hero of the day, his previous experiences over television had seemed truly exciting and promised even greater "sharing of excitement" *if only one were present.* These expectations went unfulfilled, and unfavorable comparisons with television were frequent. To present the entire body of evidence bearing on the inadequate release of tension and the widely felt frustration would be to discuss data of little relevance to televised politics. But the information collected offers unequivocal proof of a great let-down, a feeling that nothing had really happened.

The observer records show that some people voiced disappointment only because, after waiting so long, they had somehow failed to see MacArthur. Others—and such remarks were frequently part of the small talk in the crowd—thought "they ought to have a band to liven things up a little." "Heck of a parade. It's too quiet."

"They should have more music," ventured another; whereas a third person would proclaim, upon seeing the jets overhead, "Yes, that's it. We need more planes for this celebration." Disappointment centered on the failure to provide a show, not only the brevity of the peek at MacArthur. For example, a movie camera fan voiced his hope that "the next time *something* happened" he would have better luck getting pictures. "Was that a parade? Heck, I expected more than that," another disappointed spectator remarked after it was all over.

Not all of the people thought the show unrewarding, however. A participant at Soldier Field said, "It was swell. I just love crowds anyway." Those in search of excitement sometimes managed to find it. They "got a bang out of the passing police cars"; they expressed awe at the jets; or they found the throwing of confetti from office windows amusing. The opportunity to express their disregard of traffic authorities by overflowing into State Street just as soon as MacArthur had passed was another source of satisfaction for many.

Those who arrived in a "holiday spirit" were in no mood to be disappointed and ready to substitute other diversions. In one bar, two observers found a group of firemen, who had been called out as auxiliaries, engaging in mutual horseplay and collective ridicule of the entire proceedings and the set-up behind it. Restaurants were crowded, with people forming lines out into the street. Observers indicated that a "fair" proportion of those who were evidently not downtown office workers appeared "dressed for the occasion." Movie seats were, indeed, not to be had within minutes after the parade. Others found solace in the "historicalness" of the event: its like had never occurred before in Chicago. The crowds on V-E Day and for Truman during the 1948 election campaign had not been as tremendous, so spectators repeatedly commented. The spectacle, moreover (as one man told an observer), was far more lively than the Shriners' parade a year or so before, though that parade had had "real color." A woman anticipating the bridge ceremony relived her travels for the benefit of people around her and came to wonder why she had never been to the Mardi Gras in New Orleans. Even those who were abjectly disappointed consoled themselves that the weather had been good.

A Good Show on Television

For televiewers the story was different. Persons who followed the coverage saw and heard exactly what they expected to see. Here is what was shown and described by the announcer, as reported by the monitors:

> The scene at 2:50 P.M. at State and Jackson was described by the announcer as the "most enthusiastic crowd *ever* in our city. . . . You can feel the tenseness in the air . . . you can hear that crowd roar." The crowd was described by the commentator as pushing out into the street with the police trying to keep it in order, while the camera was still focusing on MacArthur and his party. The final picture was of a bobbing mass of

> heads as the camera took in the entire view of State Street northward. To the monitor, this mass of people appeared to be pushing and going nowhere. And then, with the remark, "The whole city appears to be marching down State Street behind General MacArthur," holding the picture just long enough for the impression to sink in, the picture was suddenly blacked out.

One of our monitors reported her own reaction to this phase of the television transmission:

> . . . the last buildup on TV concerning the "crowd" (cut off as it was abruptly at 3:00 P.M.) gave me the impression that the crowd was pressing and straining so hard that it was going to be hard to control. I first thought, "I'm glad I'm not in that," and "I hope nobody gets crushed."

An observer, on the scene at the moment it appeared from the TV picture that the crowds were surging out into State Street and breaking into the parade, gave the following account of what happened:

> [As MacArthur passed] everybody strained but few could get a really good glimpse of him. A few seconds after he had passed most people merely turned around to shrug and to address their neighbors with such phrases: "That's all." "That was it." "Gee, he looks just like he does in the movies." "What'll we do now?" Mostly teen-agers and others with no specific plans flocked into the street after MacArthur but very soon got tired of following as there was no place to go and nothing to do. Some cars were caught in the crowd, a matter which, to the crowd, seemed amusing.

This comparison of the television perspective with that of the participants indicates that the video treatment of MacArthur Day *preserved* rather than upset previously held expectations. Television remained true to form. From the beginning to the very end of the broadcast, it interpreted what happened in line with these expectations. Viewers received no hint of any disappointment or let-down experienced by the crowd.

Thus, on television, viewers watched MacArthur's plane land and then followed the general and his family as he was greeted by Mayor Kennelly and other dignitaries. They saw him acclaimed and greeted by "enthusiastic" crowds. But among those actually at the airport, only those fortunate few who spotted where the plane landed were able to catch a fleeting glimpse of the hero, and of his wife, as each emerged. They had to guess at what was going on during the greeting protocol. Said one girl who had been waiting to spot the general, "He's probably babbling or giving a speech." A sizable number of people—including three of the six observers who expected to watch the arrival from the airlines' observation deck—saw nothing at all. This being in the days before the ubiquitous transistor radio, they had no announcer to tell them they were waiting in the wrong place. Only the salvo given in official salute and the cheering that sounded faintly in the distance told them that the general had arrived. People near one observer were saying that "surely he would drive out of the airport their way." But gunsmoke and a plane in the distance were all they saw of MacArthur Day:

> Ours was a disappointed crowd. They were cold. They had been entertained while waiting by the arrival and departure of aircraft. The waiting period did not seem too long because of this. Excitement built up only a few minutes before twelve. This is the time at which I came to watch the sky closely and figured that there was only one way for an aircraft to land. I had expected an announcement and none had come. The guns brought the message that MacArthur had arrived. Now no one cheered; no one was happy, because the arrival was a disappointment. It meant that we had waited in the wrong place with perhaps a thousand others. The rapidity with which the crowd broke up was fascinating. . . . Disappointment was expressed by a shrug, by a grunt, and by their rapid departure.

The Structure of the TV Presentation

Television's picture of activity in the Loop continued to conform to expectations already disseminated over the mass media. Even during the early phases of the telecast, when the crowd was just beginning to gather and little was happening, television personnel were already interpreting the crowd's motivations in accordance with their own preconceptions. Later they seized on anything that could be interpreted as enthusiasm. What television failed to catch entirely was the growing disappointment of the spectators. From beginning to end, television interpreted the event true to formula, that is, as dramatic, as colossal, and as personal tribute.

The television perspective was different from that of any spectator in the crowd. Relatively unlimited in the mobility of its cameras, it could arrange events in its own way, using close-ups for what it deemed important and leaving the apparently unimportant for the background. There was almost complete freedom to aim cameras in accordance with "news" judgments. Moreover, the producer could shift to any camera that appeared to show something interesting. In this way, the technical possibilities of the medium itself helped to play up the dramatic at the expense of the routine. While the spectator, if fortunate, caught a brief glimpse of the general and his family as they passed, the televiewer found MacArthur the continuous center of attraction from his first appearance during the parade down State Street, at 2:21 P.M. until the sudden blackout at 3:00 P.M. For almost forty minutes, not counting his seven-minute appearance earlier in the day at the airport and his longer appearance at Soldier Field that evening, the TV viewer could fasten his eyes on the general and on what could be interpreted as the interplay between a heroic figure and his "enthusiastic" admirers. The cheering of the crowd seemed not to die down at all, and even as the telecast ended, the cheering seemed only to have reached its crest. The cameras focused principally on the parade itself, so the crowd's applause seemed all the more ominous a tribute from the background.

The shots of the waiting crowd, the television interviews with persons within it, and the announcers' commentaries had previously prepared the viewer for dramatic developments. The outcome was left to the inference of the individual. But television had already offered enough clues to leave little doubt about the course things were to take.

The daytime coverage of MacArthur Day lasted three hours. For over two of these MacArthur was outside the range of the camera. This time had to be filled with visual material and vocal commentary. By far the largest portion of it was spent on anticipatory shots of the crowd. Nevertheless, the relative amount of time spent watching MacArthur, as opposed to the time spent anticipating his arrival, was much greater for the TV observer than for the spectator on the scene.

Television used this waiting period to build up the viewer's expectations. The parade schedule (that is, reports on the progress of the still invisible motorcade and MacArthur's expected time of arrival) was reviewed altogether forty-five times. Reference to it took up seventeen and a half minutes of the three-hour telecast. And while these references had the character of objective reports and enabled the viewer to maintain an overall picture of the event, they nonetheless contributed to the build-up.

Televised interviews likewise had this quality of "objective" reporting. They served for the most part to elicit the expectations of spectators, but could not yet show some of their disappointment. The criterion that seemed to govern the choice of interviewees and the choice of questions was in line with the public interpretation. Thus, out of twenty-six interviews, eight were with official or semi-official personages, who in their capacity as sponsors presented the welcome as a non-political outpouring of gratitude. Five others were with army men, several of whom had served on General MacArthur's staff. Thirteen were with civilians involved as mere spectators.

Interviews with officials all stressed that on this unique and great occasion Chicago was not to be outdone. Chicago had a Democratic administration, so that "officially" MacArthur Day was entirely non-political and a matter for civic, rather than partisan, pride. The three police officials interviewed on TV emphasized especially the problems involved in controlling the spectators, as if there were a universal expectation that the crowds would get out of hand. There were also interviews with Mayor Kennelly, a representative of the mayor, the president of the Gold Star Mothers who was to participate in the bridge dedication ceremony, the Father of Prayers at the same ceremony, and former Mayor Carter N. Harrison, who was emphatic that certainly not since Admiral Dewey had Chicago seen the like of this. Among the thirteen civilians selected, four were veterans who were encouraged to state whether they had ever served under MacArthur—thus, by indirection, stressing a sentimental association with the event. Two of these thirteen were out-of-towners, a much higher proportion than our observers were able to locate.

As far as the general tone of the interviews was concerned, one observer noted while watching, "None of them really say anything, because the announcer asks questions, answers them, and the interviewees merely nod confirmation."

The descriptions by the commentators (also reflected in the interviews) determined the structure of the TV presentation of the day's events. The magnitude of the event, in line with preparations announced in the newspapers, was constantly emphasized. The most frequent theme was that "no effort has been spared to make this day memorable" (eight references). There were seven claims by announcers that they had "never seen the equal of this moment," or that it was "the greatest ovation that this city has ever turned out." The unique cooperative effort of TV was elaborated on five different occasions and was of course tied in with the "dramatic" proportions of the event.

Categorization and tabulation of every description was impossible. Guesses ranged all the way from the overcrowded transportation facilities and numerical estimates of the crowd to the length of the city's lunch hour and the state of "suspended animation" into which business had fallen. Nothing, the commentators said repeatedly, was being allowed to interfere with the success of the celebration; even the baseball game had been canceled. (But the day's activities at a nearby race track were not. When at one point in the motorcade from the airport to the Loop, a temporary traffic block resulted in a "captive audience," an irritated captive remarked, "I hope this doesn't make me late for the races.")

In addition to factual fill-ins on the parade schedule, who was who, and the focus of the shots, two—and only two—aspects of the spectacle were stressed: the unusual nature of the event and the tension which was said to pervade the entire scene. Even the eleven references to the friendly and congenial mood of the waiting crowd portended something of the change that was expected to occur. Of nine references to the orderliness, seven were in the context of "control" and police action. Four references cited the patience of the crowd, as if it were about to end.

But with regard to the crowd mood, the general emphasis was on tension and not on patience or congeniality. Twenty times the announcer was explicit about such tension, whereas, in contrast, observers' reports failed to affirm that such a mood was in any way dominant. The announcer frequently made use of phrases such as "the air is electric," "there is the feeling you just can't wait," "never such a thrill," and so forth. These descriptions went much beyond what was shown on TV, but as the crowd mood could only be inferred, the announcer had a free hand in making the event appealing to the viewer. When there was little confetti in the air, "people were saving it" so that, the announcer predicted, during the parade it might black out the TV picture. If the crowd was well in hand, the viewer was reminded that in other cities this had not been so. The size of the police detail was repeatedly reported; the many boarded windows were taken as an omen, and the references to the bodyguard, whose presence was routine, took on its own peculiar significance in such a context. Thus, in addition to direct references, the mood of the crowd was described in many subtle ways. The "happy enthusiasm" and "ardor" (three references) with which the crowd gave its greeting might have brought a sigh of relief to those anticipating "disorder"; and the cheering from the background could be interpreted as an overwhelming demonstration.

The television coverage also had a "personalizing" effect by focusing on MacArthur while allowing the background to remain obscure. This gave the TV viewer an extended opportunity to observe many little details about the general. Through television, the "very famous MacArthur wave" (the personal idiosyncrasy most frequently attributed to him during the telecast) joined the "scrambled-eggs cap" and the "battered trench coat," made famous by newspapers, as symbols visually associated with him. The already legendary charm and grace of Mrs. MacArthur also came in for mention. Yet, even MacArthur, who in the public mind (according to our observers' records) stood for a sober, austere, and heroic figure, could not hide an occasional smile from the camera. The announcers picked this up and interpreted it as the general's personal reaction to the reception. In this same way, his every move was under observation and enhanced by the commentary. MacArthur's gestures became as familiar as those of a film hero. Women could see him as a family man; see him, as a loving husband, kiss his wife during the evening ceremonies; and observers noted that these incidents (especially the kiss) received much voluble and favorable comment in places of public viewing. At such points in the telecast. the spectacle was obscured by this personal dimension.

In view of the selectivity of the coverage, with its emphasis on close-ups, it was possible for each viewer to see himself in a *personal* relationship to the general. For instance, during conversations overheard in bars with television,[2] people judged the appropriateness of MacArthur's behavior, his physical fitness (his failure to show fatigue), his family; they searched for a sign of humility or resentment on his face, a hint of gratitude at the reception or outward signs of the egotism and haughtiness imputed to him by his detractors. As the announcer shouted out, "Look at that chin! Look at those eyes!", each viewer, regardless of what the announcer meant him to look at, could seek a personal interpretation which expressed for him the real feeling underlying the exterior that appeared on the television screen.

It is against the background of this personal inspection that the significance of the telecast must be interpreted. The cheering crowd, this "seething mass of humanity," was fictionally endowed by the commentators with the same capacity for a direct and personal relationship with MacArthur as the one which television momentarily established for the TV viewer through its close-up shots. The overall effect of the televised

2. Since in 1951 far fewer people had television sets, bars were for many the place to watch television.

event thus stemmed from a convergence of these two phenomena: the seemingly extraordinary scope, including the apparent enthusiasm of the public, and the *personalizing* influence just referred to. The spectacle was interpreted in a very personal nexus. The total effect of so many people, all shouting, straining, cheering, waving a personal welcome to the general, disseminated the impression of a universal, enthusiastic, overwhelming ovation for MacArthur and all he stood for. The selectivity of the camera and the emphases of the commentary gave the televised event a *personal* dimension, nonexistent for the participants in the crowd. It was a highly unique perspective, in sharp contrast to "being there."

Other Exaggerations

Television confirmed expectations that the entire city would come to a standstill on MacArthur Day, but observer estimates of the crowd size and of the extent of disruption cast doubt on media reports that the millions of Chicagoans in the Loop might have been joined by as many as a million others who had poured into the city from the suburbs and adjoining states. For a further check on the discrepancies between the participant and television perspective, we used a number of indices to determine whether crowds and crowding were as expected: passenger statistics (obtained from the Chicago Transit Authority and suburban lines), spot checks in offices, restaurants, and parking lots, and the volume of sales reported by street vendors.

The results all substantiated the finding that MacArthur Day had been grossly blown up by the mass media. The most incontrovertible evidence came from the transit lines. The city and suburban lines reported only a very slight increase over their normal traffic loads into the city. The total increase in inbound traffic on streetcars and elevated trains was only about fifty thousand, some of this due to rerouting. The Chicago and Northwestern Railroad, a suburban service, put no additional cars on its trains. It estimated that passenger traffic was between 7 and 10 per cent above normal, mainly wives and children joining the normally "male" traffic. The additional load of some three thousand persons was easily handled within the morning rush-hour schedule. In contrast, the period between one and two o'clock in the afternoon (when the parade was going on) saw a tremendous increase over the normal load for that hour, but it was a rush *away* from the city. The railroad therefore advanced its normal rush-hour schedule by three hours, and the trains at the usual rush hour ran as they normally would have during the earlier hours. Obviously, most people who commuted regularly to the city had returned home as soon as their offices released them. A railroad official thought, based on the figures, that in fact practically all who saw the parade were Chicagoans. The same story was told by statistics from the Illinois Central, serving the southern suburbs, and from the Chicago Motor Coach Company.

These relatively slight increases in passenger traffic on public conveyances may have been nothing more than the result of fewer private automobiles that came into the city that day. Warnings by the Chicago Motor Club not to drive into the city were apparently well heeded. Our spot checks of parking lots showed that several which were normally overcrowded had a below-capacity load.

Checks at hotels indicated no unusual crowding. The influx from "out of town" failed to materialize. The YMCA, braced for an unusual demand for rooms, reported vacancies. Observations in downtown offices further confirmed orientations which the media perspective did not acknowledge. Among the office staffs sampled, only a small proportion indicated that they intended to watch the parade, even though dismissed early for the purpose. Many office workers simply took advantage of the opportunity to catch up on their shopping or household chores, including some who, on previous occasions, had been outspoken in support of MacArthur and his views.

Business in parade souvenirs was far from brisk. Hawkers, who as professional paradegoers are rather sensitive judges of enthusiasm, called the parade a "puzzler." In spite of their aggressive sales lines, they had made few sales. One observer at different times took samples of fifty persons along one block on State Street; among those walking in the space between those leaning against buildings and those pressed against the curb, there was not a single button. Among those who were evidently *spectators,* 10 per cent wore MacArthur insignia on their lapels. Another observer made extensive spot checks on sales. At the end of the parade, one vendor said, "Business is lousy in buttons and flags. Up to now I haven't sold ten buttons." A Negro vendor said that "business has been fair. Nothing like Lindbergh." Two observers working independently wrote that in their vicinity the price of buttons had dropped from 50 to 25 cents even before the end of the parade.

The purchase and display of patriotic and political symbols is another indication of whether or not people in the crowd meant, by their presence, to demonstrate their solidarity with MacArthur in the controversy that led to his dismissal and return to the States. Besides buttons, pennants, corncob pipes, and head bands, hawkers had for sale "five-star" flags. Of the fifty with which he had started out, one vendor said, he had sold all but four. Actually, these were Confederate flags, but hawkers and buyers often thought they were pennants especially designed for a five-star general. This is significant in explaining the difference in the "atmosphere" experienced by our observers and the climate as reported by the mass media. Thus, CBS Washington correspondent Charles Collingwood, on a regular newscast on April 19, had pointed to the "prevalence of Confederate flags" at MacArthur homecoming parades, which, he said, outnumbered the Stars and Stripes. Collingwood's interpretation failed to recognize that to most people the five-star flag seemed a special and fitting souvenir of the occasion. Instead he assumed that the choice of this symbol was deliberate and deduced from it that the MacArthur demonstrations derived their fervor from the opportunity for the expression of all forms of discontent and dissident views.

Detailed Illustration of the Contrast

The wreath-laying ceremony provides a graphic illustration of the contrast between the television experience and direct participation in the MacArthur welcome. The parade was scheduled to halt at only one spot, the Bataan-Corregidor Bridge. At a tri-cornered site near the entrance to the bridge, a platform had been erected. Here General MacArthur was to place a wreath under the memorial plaque, make a brief speech, and be greeted by a contingent of Gold Star Mothers. Seven of our observers were witness to the ceremony.

> *TV perspective:* In the words of the announcer, the bridge ceremony marked "one of the high spots, if not *the* high spot of the occasion this afternoon. . . . The parade is now reaching its climax at this point."
>
> The announcer, still focusing on MacArthur and the other participating persons, took the opportunity to review the ceremony about to take place. . . . The camera followed and the announcer described the ceremony in detail. . . . The camera focused directly on the general, showing a close-up, as he removed his hat and bowed his head during the invocation. He made a few remarks, looked very grave. "Those men who died were mine. I shall always hold them in my heart, inviolate and sacred. To their mothers and families who are here, I can only say that since they fell I have shared their sorrow."
>
> "Thank you, general," added the announcer. . . . There were no shots of the crowd during this period. But the announcer filled in. "A great cheer goes up at

> the Bataan Bridge, where the general has just placed a wreath in honor of the American boys who died at Bataan and Corregidor. You have heard the speech. . . . the general is now walking back. . . . the general now enters his car. This is the focal point where all the newsreels—frankly, in twenty-five years of covering the news, we have never seen as many newsreels gathered at one spot. One, two, three, four, five, six. At least eight cars with newsreels rigged on top of them, taking a picture that will be carried over the entire world, over the Chicagoland area by the combined network of these TV stations of Chicago, which have combined for this great occasion and for the solemn occasion you have just witnessed."

During this scene there were enough close-ups for the viewer to have a definite reaction, positive or negative, to the proceedings. He could see the general's facial expressions and what appeared to be momentary confusion. He could watch the activities of the Gold Star Mothers in relation to MacArthur and define this as he wished—as inappropriate for the bereaved moment or as understandable in light of the occasion. Taking the cue from the announcer, one could view the entire scene as rushed and out of line with the supremacy of the sacrifices being commemorated. But whether the event was viewed as *solemn* or not, the picture of a general being cheered—the cheer coming from an unseen crowd—while honoring the war dead could not be ignored. The cheer, whatever degree of enthusiasm it implied, had to be associated with the act and the actor just observed at close range by the televiewer. The relationship was a "personal" one, and the crowd activity, though unseen, was interpreted as similarly personal. It was possible to assume that the observer on the scene was, indeed, experiencing the same occasion.

Actually, this is the way what was meant to be a solemn occasion was experienced by those attending, an experience we call the *crowd perspective:* First, sirens were heard. Motorcycles followed by armed detachments and bands passed by. Observers differed in their accounts of the reception accorded these units in the parade. Notwithstanding the varying estimates of enthusiastic approval, the observers agreed that this was in large measure a response to the imminent arrival of MacArthur. As MacArthur's car passed, everybody pushed and strained to see. This effort to see was the major preoccupation of the crowd. In one section, people standing on crates, the only ones who could see him at all, served as "reporters" for the rest.

"There was no loud cheering in our section" when MacArthur passed, wrote one observer. "Most people waved or clapped their hands. Some people in my area didn't do anything but look and press forward." Another observer reported "little cheering, some crowding," and still another—standing some fifty feet from the second observer—indicated that "MacArthur pulled up on us rather quickly, and there seemed to be more straining to see him than cheering. . . . There were uncoordinated queries and yells heard. . . . [MacArthur] climbed the stairs and received a little more cheering and hand clapping, while the people near me were still trying to find him."

The dedication ceremony, announced as a *solemn* occasion, aroused little of the sentiment it might have elicited under other conditions. According to one observer, "People on our corner could not see the dedication ceremony very well, and consequently after he [MacArthur] had passed immediately in front of us, there was uncertainty as to what was going on. As soon as the word came that he had gone down to his car, the crowd dispersed." Another observer could not quite see the ceremony from where he was located, slightly to the east of the bridge. Condensed descriptions given by five observers illustrate the *confusion* which surrounded the actual wreath-laying ceremony:

> *The ceremony was all but over before the people realized what had happened.* While MacArthur was engaged in the ceremony, the women caught a glimpse of Mrs. MacArthur and her son. "Oh, there she is! She has a purple hat!" one shouted. The little woman beside me now pushed forward, desperately trying to see. She smiled and waved, "There's Arthur with his cap. See him?" "I wish cops didn't have heads," replied another in a jovial voice. As MacArthur was returning to the stairs, he again received an ovation. This time it seemed stronger and more united than before. He waved and some people shouted, "Hi, Mac" and "We want Mac." He got into the car and left, as the people strained to add a few inches in order to see the departing family. . . . The crowd began to disperse.
>
> It was difficult to see any of them. . . . MacArthur moved

swiftly up the steps and immediately shook hands with people on the platform waiting to greet him. There was some cheering when he mounted the platform. He walked north on the platform and did not reappear until some minutes later. *In the meantime the crowd was so noisy that it was impossible to understand what was being broadcast from the loudspeakers.* Cheering was spotty and intermittent, and there was much talk about Mrs. MacArthur and Arthur.

A car pulled up with MacArthur in it. Several people got out, one of whom was MacArthur. They all climbed up on this platform. Our view was considerably obstructed. . . . *We could catch glimpses of MacArthur speaking and hear the mumblings from the loudspeakers, but could not understand what he was saying.* . . . After he finished speaking, he walked down the steps and got a big cheer. With many exceptions, the people near me hollered hooray or something of the sort. . . . As soon as the car pulled away, everyone turned and began to walk toward Michigan, evidently hoping to get another look at MacArthur when he passed the corner of Jackson and Michigan.

Many of the people could not see him. . . . *During the dedication ceremony the general was completely out of view.* His words were amplified, but the people about me did not seem to be listening—they wanted to see him.

Those who were not on boxes did not see Mac. They did not see Mrs. MacArthur, but only her back. *MacArthur went up on the platform, as we were informed by those on boxes, and soon we heard some sound over the loudspeakers.* Several cars were standing in the street with the motors running. . . . Some shouted to the

> cars to shut their motors off, but the people in the cars did not care or did not hear. Thus the motors stayed on. The people in our area continued to push forward trying to hear. When people from other areas began to come and walk past us to go toward the train, the people in our area shrugged their shoulders. "Well, I guess it's all over. That noise must have been the speech." One of the three men who had stood there for an hour or more because it was such a good spot complained, "This turned out to be a lousy spot. I should have gone home. I bet my wife saw it much better over television."

For those on the spot, the solemnity of the occasion was thus overshadowed by the distraction of trying to catch a glimpse of MacArthur and his family. The distraction might have been less had the spectators been able to see the general. But even those who continued to try to hear could not comprehend the inarticulate sounds over the loudspeaker system. Regardless of the good intentions of the planners, solemnity was destroyed by officials in the parade intent on a time schedule and by cameramen recording the ceremony for the larger TV audience and for posterity. The witnesses often could neither see nor hear. But whether they did or not, there were few expressions of intense hero worship with overtones of nativism and political partisanship.

Instead, a crowd of disappointed spectators, cheated in their hopes of seeing a legendary figure in the flesh, was left behind.

Reciprocal Effects

There is some direct evidence for the way in which television imposed its own peculiar perspective on the event. In one case an observer at Soldier Field could watch both what was going on and what was being televised.

> It was possible for me to view the scene [at Soldier Field] both naturally and through the lens of the television camera. It was obvious that the camera presented quite a different picture from the one received otherwise. The camera followed the general's car and caught that part of the crowd immediately opposite the car and about fifteen rows above it. Thus it caught the part of the crowd that was cheering, giving the impression of a solid mass of wildly cheering people. It did not show the large sections of empty stands, nor did it show that people stopped cheering as soon as the car passed them.

In much the same way, the television viewer received the impression of wildly cheering and enthusiastic crowds before the parade. The camera selected shots of the noisy and waving audience, but in this case the television camera itself created the incident. The cheering, waving, and shouting was often but a response to the aiming of the camera. The crowd was thrilled to be on television, and many attempted to make themselves apparent to acquaintances whom they knew to be watching. Beyond that, an event important enough to warrant the most widespread pooling of television equipment in Chicago video history gained thereby in magnitude and significance. Casual conversation among the crowd continually referred to having been on television, and this was considered among the greatest thrills of the day.

The difference between the selectivity observed at Soldier Field and the "response" to the camera by the street crowds, in spite of the similar impression that resulted, is a fundamental one. The camera with its sequence of shots and its necessary commentary restructures the picture. But television equally modifies an event because of the responses it elicits. Although we had not set out to look for this second type of "structure," almost every one of the observers recorded incidents in which participants in some way addressed themselves to the television audience.

To be on television, even as one among a vast number of people, meant something to most people. They continually nudged each other and grinned, wondering what kind of image they might relay along a coaxial cable.

> A camera truck came by with the lens pointing directly at us. The Roman Catholic priest said, "Now we're going to be on television."

Such interchanges occurred often. Television entered people's consciousness in other ways. Sometimes cameras helped the crowd to orient itself to important happenings they could infer only from the direction in which the TV camera focused. Some people chose their vantage point for the chance it offered to be on TV:

> A small group of people gathered around the TV apparatus on the sidewalk, but on the whole the crowd was not deeper there than along the edge of the sidewalk. However, certain arrivals . . . were heard to comment to one another that, if we go down farther, we can get into the picture.

More generally, when we say that television modified the event, we have an image of society as a network of personal and mass communications. Any new medium of communication does more than simply "transmit" knowledge and information. Once it enters consciousness, it affects the relationships among those who use it. These effects are "reciprocal." The cheering into the camera and the choice of positions within the "beam" of the television camera illustrate this kind of effect in its most primitive form. The timing and exact scheduling, the haste with which the various ceremonies—at the airport and the bridge—were run through, and the complete inflexibility of the route suggest the staging of the event for the benefit of radio and television time schedules. The event televised was no longer the same event as it would have been had television not been there.

The "reciprocal effects" we were able to document on this occasion were admittedly scanty. At the time, the idea that they occurred was still somewhat novel. Since MacArthur Day it has become increasingly common to schedule the climax of live ceremonies or political rallies at prime TV time. Does the televising of such events cause a decline in attendance? This proposition, like most such propositions, would be difficult to prove. One thing is clear, however: an event may gain a new "public" *because* of its large television audience, even though watching it and "being there" are not the same thing. Attendance becomes a distinction precisely because so many televiewers are aware of the event. The effects are, indeed, reciprocal.

Political Perceptions and the Landslide Effect

Among the things MacArthur Day made us question was whether public moods were being accurately conveyed by television. News and special events, unlike most other television programs, represent part of that basic information about "reality" that we need in order to act in concert with anonymous but like-minded persons in the political process. Our action is guided by the possibilities for success, and, as part of this constant assessment, we constantly make inferences about public opinion as a whole. Even though most citizens acting in response to "perceived pressures" do, in fact, see only a small segment of opinion, few refrain from making estimates about the true temper. Actions and campaigns are encouraged by a feeling that they have the support of other persons. If not, these others at least constitute an action potential that can be mobilized. The evaluation of the public temper is therefore of some importance; it enters the total political situation as perhaps one of the weightiest factors.

In the absence of overt expressions of public opinion, politicians may find it useful to fabricate them. They too form a stereotyped conception of "what is" and derive from it the reasonableness of their actions. The same goes for editors and others in control of the media of mass communication, who cater to what they assume to be the interests, the visual images, and the analytic scheme of the anonymous John Q. Public. Even without any reliable knowledge about these factors, the interplay of estimates which get into the newspapers, the public response to these estimates, and television features of the kind observed during MacArthur Day could set in motion a sequence of mutually reinforcing images about public opinion. And it may turn out to be the opinion that public figures take into account.

MacArthur Day will in all probability be remembered in history as it was recorded by television journalism. The picture of public opinion so conveyed was one of overwhelming support for MacArthur in his confrontation with Truman. Those who recall these events will remember that the MacArthur testimony before Congress, which lasted an entire week, to be followed by that of Acheson and Generals Marshall and Bradley, seemed like an anticlimax to the dramatic events in the streets of San Francisco, New York, and Chicago. Having held the limelight for somewhat over a month, MacArthur actually did go into military retirement. His subsequent attempts to re-enter the spotlight, or efforts by his admirers to force him back into the center of controversy, met with little success. Never again, until his death in 1964, did the general hold national attention as he had for several weeks in 1951. The conclusions we drew from our mass-observation data about the "temper of the time" appear to have been verified and the picture inadvertently drawn by the news media refuted. The official welcomes received by MacArthur were spectacles rather than political occasions.

To be sure, a false impression of public opinion, like that created by the television coverage of MacArthur Day, can always be counteracted by other indicators such as polls. But such measures appear *after* the events and do not have the same persuasiveness. Moreover, public opinion polls are likely to reflect the effects of media coverage. When people believe that other people are almost of one mind on an issue, they are less likely to register their dissent. Thus, the polls may only add to an existing impression.

MacArthur Day is but one case of the "landslide effect" that results as media coverage of events and public responses to that coverage reinforce each other. Television disseminated an image of public sentiment that was overwhelmingly in favor of the general and, by implication, his politics. This effect gathered force as it was incorporated into political strategy, picked up by other media, entered gossip, and thus overshadowed reality as it was experienced by observers on the scene.

A landslide effect is cumulative; it builds as assumptions about "reality" lead to acts that reinforce the definition of "reality." Newsmen, in planning the coverage of a public event, make certain assumptions about their medium, about what viewers expect, and about what will hold their attention. An industry that puts great stock in audience ratings wants to assure steady interest. So the MacArthur Day telecast was made to conform to the newsmen's notions of viewers' expectations. In line with the assumed pattern, the commentators steered clear of political issues and avoided offending any viewer. Viewers were expecting a dramatic occasion, so drama it had to be, even at the expense of reality. Camera, commentary, and, to some extent, the spectators' consciousness of "being on television" helped to make the television event dramatic. Two characteristics of the TV presentation enhanced the dramatic impact of what was seen and heard and thereby contributed to the misevaluation of public sentiment:

First, the depiction of the ceremonies mainly in terms of unifying patriotic rather than potentially divisive symbols left no room for the depiction of dissent.

Second, and more important, the television presentation enlarged the viewer's field of vision but not the context in which he could interpret the event. He could see the entire crowd and, from above, it appeared as an impersonal and overwhelming force hardly subject to the influence of any one person, unanimous in its enthusiasm. Unlike the spectator in the crowd who could exchange views with the five or ten people around him, the viewer was completely dependent for his understanding of the crowd mood on what he saw and on what the commentator said. He could be everywhere the general was and see the responses to the general at every point along the parade route. His was a unique perspective. Riding with the general along the crowded parade route, he experienced the hero's welcome. He saw a mass of humanity pushing and rushing to get near the general. But he never got the true picture from television of what it meant to be a bored and often disappointed spectator who had come out to participate in an exciting and historic occasion.

III

THE TELEVISED CONVENTIONS: 1952

The Republican and Democratic party conventions held in Chicago between July 7 and July 26, 1952, were the first genuine "television" conventions. To be sure, earlier proceedings had been recorded by the TV cameras. There had been an experimental telecast of the 1940 Republican convention; the Democratic convention held in Philadelphia in 1948 had also received partial coverage, but the audience was limited to those within receiving range of the TV signal—its size was estimated at a mere one and a quarter million. Hence, the nominating conventions of 1952 set new precedents in that they were the first telecast *in their entirety* over a national hookup and viewed, according to claims by the networks, by some 65 to 70 million people.

These conventions were to become a proving ground for producers, reporters, cameramen, and politicians. None of the networks appears to have fully anticipated the long hours it was to spend on the air. Of the three networks, only ABC had committed itself in advance to cover the proceedings from "gavel to gavel"; CBS had said it would carry a minimum of twenty hours of each convention and NBC that it would carry at least thirty. Ultimately, all the networks stayed with the proceedings far longer than they had bargained for. Several sessions lasted into the early hours of the morning; one (during the Democratic convention) went nonstop for fourteen hours while all three networks stayed with it. No network, so it seemed, dared to cut away from the conventions for very long while its competitors were carrying the proceedings. As a consequence, *all* networks not only offered full gavel-to-gavel coverage, but they also provided briefings before and usually after each official session. In addition, all covered considerable portions of the hearings before the Credentials Committees, hearings conducted partly before the conventions had officially convened and partly while they were in recess. The entire coverage of the Republican convention extended on each network to approximately seventy hours; that of the Democratic to seventy-seven.

The convention telecasts underlined what was at the time called the "miracle" of television—its ability to bring the political arena directly into the home. It was widely agreed that "the television audience saw more of the conventions than the average delegate—who, like the soldier on the battlefield, could only grasp the event which occurred near to him." [1] The networks congratulated themselves on a job well done. Thus, the Radio Corporation of America advertised in the *New York Times* on August 19, 1952, some weeks after the conventions: "With the aid of television, we had what amounted to the biggest town meeting ever held . . . 60 million people had front-row seats and got a better picture of what was going on than any delegate or any reporter on the convention floor. . . . Because of television, American citizens will be better informed than they ever were before. . . . They will be able to vote for men and principles, and not for party labels."

But television was not simply a passive transmission device. Its presence entered the consciousness of the convention in many ways both before and during the proceedings. Thus, Chicago had been chosen as the convention city with an eye to allowing audiences on both coasts to watch the evening sessions at hours consistent with normal time schedules. Likewise, the conventions were held at the International Amphitheater, which was chosen in preference over a larger hall not

1. David G. Williams, "Choosing Presidential Candidates," *Political Quarterly*, XXIII (October–December, 1952), 368.

only for its better air conditioning, but especially because of its more adequate facilities for televising. During the convention, the proceedings were altered in a number of obvious and not so obvious ways. For example, the Democrats, having found that officials' activities in focus behind the speaker's rostrum distracted considerably from what any given speaker was saying to the television audience, introduced a screen shutting these activities out of view. The presence of television was invoked by several convention speakers, and campaign managers were happy to have themselves interviewed whenever it seemed to suit their purposes. Many delegates (and press reporters) used TV to keep themselves informed.

The experience with the 1952 conventions helped set the style for the televising of future political conventions. Then, and ever since, the three major networks—ABC, CBS, and NBC—pooled their coverage of the main proceedings. Six cameras of the pool were placed inside the hall, three of them facing the speaker's platform and three the crowd within the convention hall. Two other cameras were parked at the entrance to the hall, where they could catch delegates and candidates as they arrived. A single pool director made the decision as to which of the images from the pool would be available to networks at any time.

How such camera selections can result in the refraction of an event was discussed in connection with MacArthur Day and need not be reiterated here: the pooled coverage helped make that event witnessed over television considerably different from the same event experienced by participants (Chapter II). During the political conventions, however, the common coverage extended only to the *video* coverage, with pool cameras under the supervision of a single director. In addition to its contribution of equipment and personnel to this pool, each network brought with it to Chicago its own contingent of commentators, reporters, and technicians. It was through the deployment of personnel and equipment outside the common pool that a network could display ingenuity and initiative. In the first place, each network developed its own sources of information. Even when two networks were transmitting the identical picture, their interpretive comments might diverge considerably. In the second place, editors in the network studio always had the choice of substituting video transmitted from their own cameras. Thus, networks were free to insert interviews from within their own studios or from any one of the many hotel suites and lobbies into which their camera crews were able to gain entry; they could focus on activities and demonstrations in lobbies or outside the Amphitheater. They could scan the convention floor from cameras in their own booths high above the convention floor and zero-in on particular individuals, usually when they were being buttonholed by their own network reporters. With their mobile equipment they could even go right onto the convention floor for special pictures without disrupting the proceedings. For example, NBC put much stock in what it called its "walkie-lookie," a battery-operated camera, a newly designed TV version of the familiar walkie-talkie.

In the televising of any public event, a network's decisions on how to deploy its own equipment, its commentary, and the extent to which it stays with the pool and the main proceedings or substitutes "sideshows," are apt to exhibit some pattern. This pattern reflects the network's policy, while the specific decisions contain clues to its operating code. Decisions based on cultural definitions of propriety, on professional self-images of TV personnel as members of the press, or on the inherent capabilities and limitations of equipment will result in similarities among the networks. At the same time, different images of the audience (whether correct or not) and differences in organization, skill, resources, and so forth will inject idiosyncratic elements into the coverage. Each network selects camera shots and fills in with comment that stamps its own mark on the finished product. Consequently, the televising of the 1952 political conventions gave us an opportunity to study the impact of decisions on the television image of the event.

For this kind of analysis we had available three main sources of data. The first consisted of a record of the TV content of each network, based on tape recordings of the commentary and minute-by-minute descriptions by monitors of the video image. Second, we had interview information from a panel of viewers representing a wide range of socioeconomic backgrounds. These interviews, held in Chicago, were conducted within the week following each convention. They consisted of open-ended responses to queries about each convention and about specific episodes within it. Third, we had running comments and interpretations by our own monitors on developments and events in the conventions. All of our monitors were graduate students in either sociology or political science. Their on-the-spot comments represented their understanding at the particular time of what they were witnessing. Although we also had some observers in the galleries of the Amphitheater and at places of public TV viewing (for instance, bars), our coverage from these vantage points was too spotty to permit any systematic analysis.

The analysis of effects that follows, it seems to us, can only make sense to the reader if he is first reminded of relevant episodes that occurred during each of the conventions. Thus, our explanation is prefaced with a brief account of the proceedings. We have tried to limit these sketches to the basic, uncontested "facts." The reader interested in a more detailed account can consult the published proceedings of each convention as well as the study by Paul David and his associates.[2]

The Republican Convention

The convention that met from July 7 through July 11 and nominated General Dwight D. Eisenhower as its presidential candidate was involved in a bitter dispute

2. Paul T. David, Malcolm Moos, and Ralph M. Goldman, *Presidential Nominating Politics in 1952*, Washington, D.C., Brookings Institution, 1954.

between two wings of the Republican party. Since Eisenhower was subsequently elected, and re-elected, by a very substantial margin, many may not know or have forgotten how touch-and-go his nomination was, how exciting was the balloting at the convention, how intricate were the events and maneuvers by which Eisenhower emerged as the victor at the Chicago convention.

The contest at the Amphitheater, whose outcome was witnessed by the TV audience, had been squarely joined for some months. Both Eisenhower and his opponent, Senator Robert A. Taft of Ohio, who had earned for himself the name of "Mr. Republican," came to Chicago with sufficient support to sense victory. What transpired during the five days of the Republican convention represented only the resolution of developments that had been in process for some time.

Eisenhower had been one of the most popular World War II military heroes, but unlike MacArthur his popularity had not been linked with any particular political persuasion. It was essentially nonpartisan.[3] He had been widely discussed as a possible candidate for both the Democratic and the Republican tickets in 1948. In the spring of 1952, after nearly a year of uncertainty during which it was not at all clear whether or not Eisenhower would even accept a "draft," he was finally induced to resign his position as supreme com-

3. Hyman and Sheatsley, "The Political Appeal of President Eisenhower," cited in Chapter II.

mander of NATO forces in Europe in order to come home and campaign actively for the Republican nomination. His "active seeking of the position" was necessitated by Senator Taft's evident success in a systematic quest for delegates. By early summer the senator had pledges for something like 550 votes of the 604 he would need to win.

The support Taft enjoyed among Republican stalwarts, particularly in the Midwest, had enabled him to wrest control of the Republican party organization from Governor Thomas E. Dewey of New York, the man who twice before, in 1944 and 1948, had suffered defeat in the presidential election. Taft had used his control of the party machinery to install his own supporters as key convention officials. Hallanan was selected to be Temporary Chairman, to be replaced by Martin as Permanent Chairman as soon as the convention was properly constituted. Taft's friends predominated among the speakers, and General MacArthur, a long-standing opponent of Eisenhower, was to give the "keynote" address. Similarly, Taft supporters appeared to be in firm control of the Credentials Committee, which had to pass on the rights of all delegates to be seated at the convention, and of the Platform Committee responsible for the drafting of the party program.

As far as Taft's opponents were concerned, his success in corralling pledges and delegations and his use of the convention machinery constituted a "steamroller." It had to be stopped, and the opportunity to do so seemed to present itself when the Taft forces moved into Texas to round up a delegation that would support the senator from Ohio.

It is well known that at the time the Republican party in most Southern states was almost nonexistent between elections. It surfaced every four years primarily to play a role in the selection of a presidential nominee and, because of its normal shadowy existence, was usually torn by factional strife over who was properly entitled to represent the wishes of the constituencies at the national convention. The Taft forces were able to win out in Texas, even though the Eisenhower candidacy had considerable popular support from a large group of voters who, though previously registered as Democrats, were politically closer to the Republicans and ready to convert if Eisenhower were the candidate. Some of these voters spearheaded the Eisenhower campaign in Texas. The issue at the state convention, held at Mineral Wells, revolved around the eligibility of the Johnny-come-lately Eisenhower supporters to help select the instructed delegates. The Eisenhower forces made effective use of the mass media and helped focus attention on proceedings that ordinarily were of little more than local interest. When a slate of delegates favoring Taft won out, the Eisenhower managers had their issue. They called the outcome a "theft of delegates" and sent Eisenhower into Texas to call for "fair play."

"Fair play" in this context had a very specific meaning, one that was often lost on the public. The issue was whether members of this disputed delegation (and of other delegations whose credentials were challenged) were entitled to vote upon the credentials of other delegates whose accreditation by the Taft-controlled committee might be challenged from the convention floor. Precedent was clear only on their ineligibility to vote on the matter of their own seating. However, the point was effectively made clear by Dewey and other campaign managers in the Eisenhower camp: if these disputed delegates could vote on any other dispute, this would not be "fair play." By chance, the annual meeting of governors of the forty-eight states took place in Texas shortly after the Republican state convention. Under Dewey's leadership, the pro-Eisenhower governors succeeded in soliciting a call from other Republican governors for a "fair-play" amendment to the rules of the national convention.

In Chicago, the first forum to hear the case for the disputed delegations was the Taft-dominated National Committee. When the committee refused to open its hearings to television, a political scientist wrote: "The Eisenhower commanders simply stood aside while the new but powerful television industry, jealous of its rights, turned its full rage upon the committee. The din was so great that most Americans undoubtedly felt that an effort was being made to hold the hearings in secret. Actually they had always been open to the press. The Taft majority in this case were old-fashioned rather than malicious; one Taft official complained,

'Next thing we know they'll bring a printing press into the committee room.' "[4]

The issue of the "Texas steal" and "fair play" raised by the Eisenhower forces led to an important concession even before the convention got under way. Sixteen of thirty-eight Texas delegates were conceded to Eisenhower, and there were reports that in an effort to avoid a showdown there had been an offer of further concessions, in a conference just behind the speaker's platform, just about the time the convention and the convention telecast were to start.

The convention itself was a clear two-way contest that involved two tests of strength, as a result of which the outcome of the one and only ballot for the nomination became successively more predictable. The first test vote came at the opening session on Monday, July 7, when Governor Langlie of Washington, an Eisenhower supporter, offered his Fair Play Amendment asking that any delegation contested by more than one-third of the National Committee be disbarred from voting on the seating of other delegations. An amendment to this amendment was offered by Taft-man Clarence E. Brown of Ohio, whom some commentators later called the "goat" of the convention for this evident tactical blunder. He only confused the issue by calling for the exemption of seven members of the disputed Louisiana delegation whose own credentials had not been challenged under the Fair Play rule. After

4. Williams, "Choosing Presidential Candidates," p. 371.

a long debate, the Brown amendment was put to a vote and defeated. The Fair Play Amendment was passed shortly thereafter.

The case of the disputed delegations next came before the convention's Credentials Committee. In hearings which were fully televised, the Taft forces gave further ground. Nevertheless, when the final report of this committee came before the convention on Wednesday evening during the sixth session, there was a second test of strength. As a result, despite an eloquent speech by pro-Taft Senator Dirksen of Illinois, all decisions on disputed delegates by the Credentials Committee favorable to Senator Taft were reversed by a vote from the floor, and Eisenhower delegates were seated instead.

After a day of more or less routine business climaxed by the official nominating speeches and demonstrations, the convention was able to convene for balloting on Friday morning, July 11. Eisenhower was nominated on the first ballot, and Nixon was nominated as vice-presidential candidate later the same day. The Eisenhower acceptance speech was arranged for early evening, a period of prime television time.

The official ballot on the last day of the Republican convention, following, as it did, two previous test votes, was really a third rather than a first ballot for the nomination. The turning point had really come two days before, when the resolution of the seating dispute more or less determined who would win. There were, to be sure, other implications to the seating dispute. The Republican Old Guard was fighting attempts to give the party a new image; isolationists were fighting internationalists. There was also the legal and moral issue of "fair play" taken by itself. Be this as it may, the import of every vote against accepting the Credentials Committee report succeeded in moving Eisenhower nearer the nomination, irrespective of whether the vote was meant to be cast for "fair play" or for anything else. This is what the viewer had to understand.

It was also during the voting on the Credentials Committee report that some of the real drama of the convention was enacted before the television cameras. We shall now turn our attention to how some aspects of this drama were understood by viewers.

The "Mystery Man" of the Republican Convention

In July, 1952, Governor John S. Fine of Pennsylvania was for most of the viewers we interviewed as much a video-created star as pianist Liberace. Governor Fine was able to dramatize himself as a key political figure at the Republican convention. In television interviews and press conferences just before the convention, he had managed to present himself as the "mystery man" of the hour, the man who held in his pocket a large number of Pennsylvania votes. Exactly how many votes he controlled never became apparent; and which way he would choose to throw them, he just wasn't saying. Only Governor Dewey, who had obviously played an important role in the pre-convention campaign and did remain an important national figure afterward, received more mentions than Governor Fine as the most influential man at the Republican convention of 1952. Viewers most frequently mentioned as evidence of Fine's importance: "TV gave that impression," and "He controlled a big delegation." How did the TV image of Fine's influence become unduly, even though only temporarily, magnified?

There was, to begin with, a distinct parallel between the treatment of Fine's role by a particular network during the seating dispute on Wednesday night and the number of mentions he received from viewers: more than others, monitors covering the ABC telecast noted how consistent was the attention paid to Fine and his antics. The efforts of one commentator, in particular, to get a scoop by pinning the governor down on his choice, helped to turn him into the "hero of the convention." Interview records likewise indicated that viewers who followed the convention primarily on ABC most often ascribed to the governor an unusual amount of political power. Though definitions of Governor Fine's role were necessarily the product of a viewer's total experience during the week of the Republican convention, it is possible to draw some conclusions from the treatment he received on Wednesday evening. One member of our viewer sample referred to all the relevant episodes collectively as the *"night of the fight."*

Governor Fine's evening performance began at 8:05 P.M., when he made an unexpected joint-appearance, arm-in-arm with Dewey, on the convention floor during a routine speech by Republican House Majority Leader Martin. Our monitors watching the TV screen saw "people standing up in the background, *apparently* watching more important things than the speech. . . ." Among the many shots of people and objects caught by the camera as it scanned the convention floor was a brief glimpse of Governors Dewey and Fine together. Listening to Martin, the speaker, one monitor recorded that he heard him "starting to mispronounce his words, apparently controlling himself with difficulty," and that there was a "tremendous noise" in the background, a noise clearly discernible on our audio tapes. Other monitors also observed that there was no response to Martin's jokes and "hardly any reaction" to cues in his speech that ordinarily should have elicited applause.

Temporary Chairman of the Convention Walter Hallanan rapped for order. He called on the sergeant-at-arms to remove newspapermen and "everyone" from the middle aisle. One pool camera swept the hall; it caught Dewey and followed him to his seat. Six minutes later Hallanan had to interrupt once more with a call for order. Something was going on—but what?

Here are the explanations received by viewers on each network: Commentators on NBC cut in momentarily during the Martin speech to identify Dewey and Fine just as they were shown together. CBS made no comment at this time but later, after the speech was ended, told the viewer "that disturbance . . . was when Governor Fine came in with Governor Dewey arm in arm. There's a lot of political significance in that because . . . the indications are that Governor Fine has now cast in his lot definitely with General Eisenhower and this was the proof of it, so it was felt by the convention floor tonight when he and Dewey came in arm in arm." ABC made no mention of Dewey or Fine, but it told the viewer what could be seen as Hallanan rapped for order: "If you're watching your picture closely, you see that tempers are growing a little short on the rostrum and stand . . . and that feelings are growing higher down among the delegates. . . . [You'll see] in your television camera faces you'll recognize: people—delegates making last-minute deals." Later, ABC referred again to "excited" delegates and allegedly "clear signs of progress of the Eisenhower forces," yet it did not actually mention the surprising appearance of Dewey and Fine on the floor together.

NBC, the only network to identify the pair at the time they were shown on the screen, commented immediately after Martin's speech that "everyone was wondering just what they were talking about," and some ten minutes later a commentator gave an interpretive summary in which he spoke at length about the "rudeness" of the Dewey-Fine behavior. In the course of this commentary, he referred, quite incidentally and casually, to Fine as an "Eisenhower supporter," as if this were a well-known fact. CBS also, as the earlier citation indicates, recorded the implication of the joint appearance. Only ABC failed to clear up the "mystery" of Fine. Though speaking in general terms of the progress made by the Eisenhower forces, it did not indicate that the "mystery man" had evidently made up his mind.

Until this episode occurred there was indeed a residue of mystery. During the preceding afternoon session, each of the three networks had made a brief trip to the Pennsylvania caucus room. In that caucus, Fine had been outright in his refusal to commit himself publicly on his choice for the nomination, and, failing to obtain any new information, all networks had returned to the floor in short order. Sometime after the Dewey-Fine incident, ABC, the only network which had not used the occasion to clear up the mystery for its viewers, was the only network to take its viewers to the Pennsylvania caucus room just as the floor debate over the seating of the predominantly pro-Taft delegation from Georgia was about to come to a close and, presumably, to a vote.[5]

Pointing to Fine chairing the caucus meeting, the ABC announcer told the viewers: "You can be sure that the gentlemen are considering very seriously some of the things that have been said and that you have been listening to in the last half-hour. . . . [The Pennsylvania delegation is] going to caucus on the question of the minority report [favoring the seating of pro-Eisenhower delegates from Georgia]." The commentator appeared to imply that the delegation would decide on this controversial question after sober assessment of the legal

5. An observer taking notes on the reactions of a group of seven who were watching the Wednesday evening telecast on ABC summed up their feelings: "They interrupt the vote to tell the story about Fine and the Pennsylvania caucus. This is pretty bad. We want to follow the vote."

arguments advanced in the debate—an understanding that few members of our panel were inclined to share. Then, as Fine made a sudden exit from the caucus room, the viewer was told, "Pennsylvania will stand pat." The viewer got the impression that a decision on the seating had finally been reached, and Fine was hurrying to get back to the floor to record it.

Because ABC viewers were "at the caucus" and not following the floor proceedings, they were not privy to what viewers on other channels were witnessing at the same time. They missed a move by Summerfield of Michigan to recess the convention before taking a roll call on the seating of the Georgia delegation, a motion turned down by a voice vote. When ABC returned to the floor, the roll call on the acceptance of the minority report was already in progress. A series of events that amounted, in the words of one interviewee, to a "rumpus on the rostrum" followed in quick succession.

The "rumpus" began so suddenly and so unexpectedly that our monitors, ordinarily so perceptive, were altogether puzzled about what was going on. Here is what all notes more or less agreed on: As Hallanan, the Temporary Chairman, stood at the rostrum calling the roll, an angry Fine came up from behind to grab him, presumably in order to attract his attention. Fine was shouting and protesting that an agreement not to hold a roll call before there had been a chance to caucus was being violated. Hallanan, pounding his gavel, announced to the convention (and to Fine) that, whatever the agreement, a motion to recess had been put to the convention and rejected. He would therefore proceed with the roll call. Fine then left the platform. When he reached the aisle of the convention floor, the camera caught him again as he was besieged by reporters.

The ABC monitors concentrating on the picture wrote down these impressions as the episode unfolded:

> Fine almost sends his fist in the face of the chairman. Angry Governor Fine. Fine argues with the Temporary Chairman. Arguing and gesturing violently. Fine marches down the aisle—is he being ushered out? Close-up of Fine calling his men out. Fine really lets himself go before TV. See him coming down aisle with police escorts.

As unlikely a possibility as a governor being "bounced" from the convention hall presented itself to the monitors on ABC, because they had *not* witnessed Summerfield's motion, to which Hallanan had referred in his explanation. Similar speculations about unlikely possibilities were also advanced by monitors of other channels, but it was because *they* did *not* know Fine had been in the caucus room when the motion to recess was rejected, and that he had evidently come rushing to the platform when he was notified of what he believed was an abrogation of an agreement.

The confusion about the meaning of Fine's behavior was the result of viewers *on all three channels* lacking one or the other necessary piece of information. Our monitoring records contain no indication that the reason for Fine's absence from the floor at the time of the motion was ever clarified. NBC and CBS identified Fine as he suddenly appeared on the platform but otherwise let the picture speak for itself. ABC offered an interpretation that only succeeded in highlighting the obvious and thus added to the mystery.

> In order that you'll understand the discussion on the platform, Governor Fine . . . is . . . making a protest. That's Hallanan. This is a very interesting thing now. You watch it carefully. . . . Governor Fine is very indignant. Hallanan is calling for order. Now we'll see whether some previous arrangement is going to be brought up and will be changed or not.

Apparently the commentator was as uninformed about the rejection of the motion to recess as the viewers.

Fine had evidently called his men out, not—as one monitor thought—out of the convention, but to the caucus room. Nine minutes later ABC again followed him there, filling in:

> . . . just concluded an extremely dramatic meeting. . . . Fine rushed in here absolutely incensed about having been overruled on a demand for a 45-minute recess . . . announced a vote of 57 to 13 in support . . . said angrily, "If anybody wants to poll us on that, let them go ahead."

In ABC's presentation, the exact Pennsylvania vote subsequently became part of the "mystery" surrounding Governor Fine's role.

The governor's next appearance before the television audience came as he answered the roll call to cast the votes of the Pennsylvania delegation on the credentials of the Georgia delegates. Fine began to explain his earlier stage performance but was quickly interrupted by Hallanan. After some exchange, Fine cast a vote of 57 to 13 in support of the pro-Eisenhower slate but added that he had no idea whether it was correct as he had been denied his chance to caucus. Immediately there was a demand from a Pennsylvania delegate that the delegation be polled in order to verify the vote. CBS told its viewers:

> Fine alleging no opportunity to poll since an agreement was broken which should have given him time—at least that's what he's alleging. . . . Governor Fine . . . meeting with the press at one side of the hall. Anxiously awaiting poll to see whether it confirms report he gave.

NBC told its audience: "Governor Fine is upset because he was not allowed to caucus his state." ABC, continuing its emphasis on Fine as the "mystery man," said, "[We're] in the midst of another one of those extended polls. . . . [there's a] hint from Governor Fine that there may be a change in the vote."

Our monitors saw "Fine speaking in an agitated fashion" and "still mad." Wrote one: "I can't figure Fine's motives, but he doesn't seem to be acting in a responsible, rational manner."

The poll revealed that Fine's estimate of the Pennsylvania delegation's vote had indeed been wrong. But there was no mystery in this change from a vote of 57 to 13 to 52 to 17.

On CBS, Fine did not star again that evening; that is to say, a viewer watching for Fine could catch him on a number of different occasions later on, but his big part had been played. On NBC he made one more very brief appearance as a featured player in an interview. Only ABC continued to cast him in a lead role. After the vote on the question of which Georgia delegation to seat, ABC once more took its viewers to the Pennsylvania caucus room where:

> Fine is expected to read an extremely stinging statement denunciatory of what he regards now as the tactics of the Taft-dominated convention machinery. . . . [This] will perhaps start the bandwagon for Eisenhower . . . perhaps one of the historic moments of American history, for Republicans at least.

The commentator failed to suggest that with the vote in favor of seating the Eisenhower delegations the bandwagon had already begun to roll. The Pennsylvania vote on this question had already made it fully clear that Fine would under no circumstances attempt to keep the Eisenhower bandwagon from rolling by throwing his votes to Taft.

ABC viewers watching the Pennsylvania caucus heard Fine's explanation of what had taken place on the floor: he didn't blame anyone in particular for the failure to have the forty-five-minute recess; he wanted to avoid harsh words; the Republicans would have to elect as well as to nominate a President. Then Fine announced that he would vote for Eisenhower. The commentator talked about the "Eisenhower bandwagon which Fine *has just boarded.*" Thus the mystery had ended.

It is our contention that the emphasis ABC gave to the mystery of Fine, at the expense of following developments on the floor, gave viewers an exaggerated idea of Fine's power. The commentary led the viewer to focus on Fine as a "politician," and Fine's activities themselves led the viewer to form a vivid picture of his role.

To be sure, some viewers became irritated at ABC because of the forced trips to the Pennsylvania caucus room, but irritation about these caucuses was not usually directed at the network. Persons interviewed after the Republican convention often expressed annoyance at Fine "showing off," not at television "showing off" Governor Fine. They enjoyed their peeks into the "smoke-filled" caucus room and wished there had been more of them. Whether annoyed or not, most were also fascinated: they enjoyed Fine's petulant and, at the time, puzzling behavior, deplored it, and used what they perceived to make judgments about the kind of a man Fine was. If monitors—even those of ABC—did not think Fine was a mystery man and felt—as they did—that he was not important enough to rate the attention given him, most of our respondents were less skeptical. Some were "kept guessing by Fine all along."

The effect of ABC's treatment of events on the definition of Fine can be further pinpointed through the responses of viewers. One member of our panel, when asked at the beginning of an interview a few days after the convention about what stood out most in his memory, said, "I remember Governor Fine's polling for Ike." Another thought Fine got "so excited about not having a caucus" that he "tried to run the convention." Still another summed up his understanding of the series of incidents involving Fine as viewed over ABC:

> You could see what people were bitter by their actions. For example, Governor Fine when he wasn't allowed to have a caucus. You could tell Fine was bitterly, terribly disappointed at first. He became very very angry. Hallanan made Fine mad and, *because of this,* Fine threw his support to Eisenhower, switched his votes to Ike, whereas before he had been for Taft.

In its attempt to "keep it interesting" and to go "behind the scenes," either unintentionally or deliberately in order to make a good story, ABC succeeded only in distorting the picture. It withheld mention of all signs which, prior to Fine's announcement on television, had already made it clear that his intention to support Eisenhower was no mystery. On July 6, the Sunday before the convention opened, one of the pre-convention telecasts featured the "mystery man, Fine." At that time, our monitor indicated that, from his remarks, Fine had "obviously" thrown in his lot with Eisenhower. Yet the ABC newsmen elected to keep up the guessing game until the official declaration at their televised caucus.

The way Fine became a mystery man with some votes to throw around, furthermore, fitted in with certain preconceptions many viewers had of a politician in action. To them Fine appeared to be "peddling" his influence, and if the media exaggerated that influence, viewers were unaware of this distortion. Over television his actions appeared neither subtle nor difficult for the viewer to "figure out for himself." Viewers thought they could *see* that Fine was angry; they could *see* he was disappointed or bitter. And, as one interviewee put it, *"You could see it on the expression on his face and, besides, the commentator said so."*

Thus, television, with a strong assist from Fine himself (who was apparently not adverse to making news), lent a particular vividness to his role at the convention. Though five days earlier Fine had not been a nationally prominent governor, the viewer "saw for himself" Fine's influence on events. Yet the viewer's picture was somewhat out of focus, and most viewers were totally unaware of how the pursuit of Fine into the caucus room and the many interviews with him had enhanced the importance and power imputed to the Pennsylvania governor. He was no more important than any other head of a large delegation.

The Democratic Convention

Ten days after the Republicans had concluded their meetings, the Democrats opened their convention in Chicago. Meeting from July 21 through July 26, they nominated as the standard bearer of their party Governor Adlai E. Stevenson of Illinois, who until that time was practically unknown to the general public outside his own state. The viewer who had followed the Republican proceedings had the advantage of some elementary familiarity with the organization and procedures of a political nominating convention. But this apparent advantage was more than offset by differences in the major "plots" of the two conventions, particularly by the complexity of the maneuvers among the Democrats, who —it has always been recognized—manage to enjoy themselves more in being "politicians."

Where the Republican convention involved essentially a "straight fight" between two leading contenders, there were among the Democrats five persons (not counting favorite-son candidates) who came to Chicago actively seeking the nomination. There was, in addition, Stevenson, whose followers had set up campaign headquarters on the fifteenth floor of the Conrad Hilton Hotel, despite his unwillingness to do anything personally to advance his own candidacy. Whatever happened at the Republican convention could be understood simply by establishing some linkage to the two-way contest between "Ike" and Taft. From either side, it was not too difficult to define the "good guys," the villains, and the fence-sitters. Among the Democrats, however, the various lines of division on candidates and issues tended to criss-cross and shift. It was sometimes difficult to fathom the composition of any temporary coalition or to assess the implications of any vote for the fortunes of any candidate. As Richard Rovere put it, "At the Republican convention, there seemed to be something like a plausible connection between the candidates and the ideas they were supposed to stand for. Among the Democrats this year, not only at their convention but during the whole pre-convention campaign, the connections existed but they did not seem very plausible." [6]

Among the candidates actively seeking the nomination, Senator Estes Kefauver of Tennessee, star of the televised hearings on organized crime and subsequently a winner of primaries in several states, had come to the convention with the largest block of committed delegates. Senator Richard Russell of Georgia was the candidate of the South. There were also Senator Robert Kerr of Oklahoma and former Mutual Security Administrator Averell Harriman of New York, as well as the septuagenarian Vice President Alben Barkley of Kentucky, who withdrew his candidacy just before the convention when several labor leaders refused him their support because he was too old. And then there was the candidacy of Adlai Stevenson, who had never shut the door altogether on a genuine draft.

6. "Letter from Chicago," *New Yorker,* August 2, 1952, p. 50.

Shortly after the convention opened, a group of young Democrats, who came to be identified as the "liberals," began rallying support for a resolution that would require all delegates to sign a loyalty pledge as a condition to their being seated. The avowed purpose was to prevent a recurrence of what had happened in 1948, when in some Southern states Truman's name did not appear on the ballot as the Democratic party candidate. But the move was also meant to reduce the influence of these Southern conservatives in the selection of a nominee. Persons who were likely to bolt to Eisenhower, the "liberals" reasoned, should not be permitted to stymie the selection of a truly liberal candidate.

The resolution asked that delegates promise to use "all honorable means" to see that the name of the convention's nominee was on their state ballot. This wording was adopted without a roll call in the first evening session on Monday, July 21. Continued protests by some Southern state delegations who had voted against the pledge led to a further compromise. As a result of committee meetings a proviso was added that this pledge would be binding "for this convention only." Nevertheless, Virginia, South Carolina, and Louisiana still refused to sign. Early on Thursday evening, July 24, when the major but not yet the minor nominations for President had been finished, the question of the right of these states to participate in the official proceedings was raised once again and brought to a vote over the seating of the Virginia delegation. The vote was a long and drawn-out affair with many delegations asking to be polled. The turning point came after Pennsylvania and Illinois, two key delegations in which Stevenson sentiment was strong, surprisingly reversed their prior vote and decided in favor of Virginia. The trend in the vote, which at first had gone against seating, was quickly reversed as other delegations also changed their vote. South Carolina and Louisiana were seated shortly thereafter.

That same evening, those backing the loyalty pledge moved to adjourn the convention before balloting began on the nomination. Although the motion was defeated, the convention did adjourn until the next day after a fire started on the convention floor and the fire chief pointed to the hazard caused by the many newspapers and other litter strewn about.

Next day, Friday, July 25, two slow ballots, in which Kefauver, Stevenson, and Russell led the field, occupied the entire morning and afternoon. After a dinner recess, Harriman and Dever (the favorite-son candidate of Massachusetts) announced their withdrawal in favor of Stevenson. The third ballot was likewise a protracted affair, lengthened by continuous requests for polling of delegations. At the end of it, Stevenson was nominated and came to the Amphitheater to deliver his celebrated acceptance speech at so late an hour that the television audience was minimal. Senator John Sparkman of Alabama received the nomination as vice-presidential candidate the following morning.

The dispute over the loyalty pledge was the key to understanding the Democratic convention, but it was only during the roll call vote on the seating of the Virginia delegation, on Thursday evening, that its precise relationship to the fortunes of the various candidates gradually became evident. Until then it had been rare for commentators to identify a single candidate with any tactical move. Instead, interpretations of the seating dispute had relied mostly on such themes as the traditional North-South cleavage, attempts to secure unity at the convention and avoid a permanent North-South split, young and ambitious "amateur" politicians fighting the old "pros," liberals versus conservatives, an endeavor to force party loyalty on those whose affiliation with the national Democratic party appeared to be purely nominal, and improving the chances of electing a Democratic President by advance assurance that the nominee's name would appear on the ballot in all states. Only during the balloting on Thursday night did the stop-Stevenson forces begin to label the move to seat Virginia as a move *by* the Stevenson forces. The motion to adjourn, made moments later, then became a test vote between the Stevenson supporters and a temporary coalition formed by Kefauver and Harriman backers for that evening.

Yet television did not always stress the implications of these events for the outcome of the convention. Not only was there considerable confusion over the significance of what had happened on Thursday night, but the clear ascendancy of Stevenson between the second and third ballots on Friday, while the convention recessed for dinner, remained to many a puzzle. In scrutinizing how some episodes during the Democratic convention were handled by television, we shall be primarily interested not so much in the capacity of television to dramatize the role of particular individuals, but in how many disparate events are linked by commentary to affect the viewer's interpretation of those events. Through these linkages television "structures" an event. It does so even where news personnel are positively committed to objective reportage.

Chairman Rayburn and the Fight for the South

A quasi-experimental situation during the course of the Democratic seating fight supplied clear evidence that the commentary on the three television networks sharing the pooled video coverage had given, in each case, a significantly different structure to the event. As a consequence, persons watching on each of the networks got a different idea of what was going on and what to make of it. In the following pages we let the reader reach the conclusion with us that the different interpretations reflect an unwitting bias on the part of the telecasters and, further, that this bias can in part be attributed to differences in the telecasters' judgments of their audience.

The period subject to intensive analysis began at 4:56 P.M., Thursday, July 24, and lasted until 1:07 the next morning. Our analysis begins at the point during the roll call on nominations for the presidency when Louisiana, one of the states refusing to sign the so-called "loyalty pledge," yielded to its co-rebel Virginia for a parliamentary inquiry about the status of nonsigners in the convention. A ruling by the chair, that they could not vote unless they signed the pledge, was reversed after a drawn-out roll call characterized by considerable vote switching. Virginia, South Carolina, and Louisiana, the three non-complying states, were seated during this session, but not until after Senator Douglas of Illinois had started a dramatic attempt to halt the proceedings by moving for adjournment. The verbal fireworks were finally interrupted only by a genuine fire on the floor of the convention. Panic was narrowly averted by a Massachusetts delegate who seized the only open mike and "talked the fire out." After it was extinguished, the debate went on but briefly. Notwithstanding a prior defeat of the move to adjourn, just a little while after the fire another adjournment motion was suddenly recognized and quickly gaveled through.

During this period the television coverage of these episodes by the three networks was being monitored for visual and verbal content, and almost all of it was taped. In addition, monitors were encouraged to record (where and when possible) their own interpretations of what they were seeing and hearing. At the time, the monitors did not consider these periodic interpretations as data that would be subject to systematic analysis. Nevertheless, the use of these comments as data resulted in an interesting observation: *the monitors on CBS gave a significantly different evaluation of the evening's activi-*

ties than monitors on ABC and NBC. The question was, what had led to this differential "effect"?

One monitor's notes, jotted down just after the close of the session at about 2:30 A.M., summarized the conflict in interpretations: all three persons monitoring CBS thought that with his attempt to force an adjournment "Douglas had made a fool of himself." Their resentment centered on the "so-called liberals"—notably Kefauver of Tennessee—who "would do anything to stop Stevenson."

> They saw the roll call on the move to adjourn as a "test of strength" on the part of the Kefauver-Harriman forces versus Stevenson. . . . They felt that the move to keep the Dixiecrats out—at this point—was only a political maneuver on the part of the Kefauver-Harriman forces.

NBC monitors were equally resentful, but in a different way. As far as they were concerned, Rayburn and cohorts had put on a bad show . . .

> shoved the Southern states in. . . . They recognized that politics were involved, but never thought of the vote as a simple "test of strength."

A check with monitors of ABC revealed that their attention, like that of the NBC viewers, had been focused on Chairman Rayburn's part in the proceedings. They had viewed the event as the attempt of a "Stevenson-Byrnes coalition against Kefauver" to achieve "unity at any cost."

In view of the reasonable homogeneity of backgrounds and outlook among the ten monitors, the resulting differences could not be seen as the influence of individual preconceptions. Recruited from a group somewhat above the usual college age—most of them veterans of World War II, all but one working on or having obtained graduate degrees in the social sciences—they individually rated themselves politically sophisticated. This self-judgment was borne out by an evaluation of their past exposure to conventions, interest in news media, and political experience and knowledge. Being pre-convention "eggheads" (from Illinois), they were all strongly opinionated in favor of the Stevenson candidacy, with only one favoring Eisenhower over Stevenson among all possible candidates of either party.

Also "controlled" was the monitors' exposure to earlier telecasts of the Republican convention. All had had an opportunity to compare and evaluate the quality of coverage on each network. This enabled them to assess, accept, or discount the particular emphases of each. Again, the explicit monitoring instructions assured a constant and comparable amount of attention from each person. Because during the period analyzed the networks relied heavily on pooled video coverage of the floor, televiewers on the different networks were exposed for the most part to the same visual image. The effect of cutaways, since they were few and brief, should have been minimal.

It therefore seemed a legitimate assumption that significant differences in group interpretations and understanding resulted from a difference in network commentary rather than from camera choices or from distinctive frames of reference with which our monitors approached the telecasts. The inherent "open-endedness" in each of the episodes during the evening's telecast further supported this view. Being unusually complicated and full of surprising turns, they were open to varying interpretations. The commentary of each network, during the period in question, was meant to fill in the information on convention procedures and backstage developments that might help to understand the developing strategy. The differences in commentary thus reflected the telecasters' conception of what interested the audience and what they needed to know in order to follow.

Yet when we scrutinized and compared the commentary on each of the networks, we were surprised to find that neither the amount of information nor the basic facts differed in any essential way. As a result, we were led to look in a new direction, namely at the manner in which the various televised episodes were *linked* to prior events and to events outside the range of the cameras. The context so created could well account for variations in viewers' interpretations of the same events. The same overt elements could be put together into a number of different configurations.

Here is a schematic picture of how this might occur. First, the *interpretation* given to a particular incident (or the *lack of interpretation*) affects the viewer's focus of attention. Similarly, the *timing of information* also contributes to the formation of a frame of reference into which subsequent incidents are fitted. However, once this *frame of reference becomes crystallized,* it tends to overshadow subsequent information so that new and contradictory information will be ignored. A network's tone or attitude toward the convention also has certain subtle effects. We might call this the *"style" of coverage.* These elements together encourage viewers to interpret a complex and confusing event in a particular way. This structuring can occur in ways that are not only entirely unintended by network news personnel but altogether unantipicated by them as well.

An analysis, episode by episode, of how the events on the Thursday night of the Democratic convention were reported by each network, should clarify how the divergent definitions by viewers of these same events were a result of decisions that inadvertently gave these events different structures.

1. (4:56–7:30 P.M.) *The Rayburn ruling.* The seating fight really began with the calling of Louisiana, which yielded to Virginia for a parliamentary inquiry. Neither state had signed the "loyalty pledge." In answer to a request for clarification and after some wrangling, Rayburn ruled that failure to sign excluded Virginia from participation in the official proceedings.

Monitors: During this phase, all three channels let the video carry the story. Monitors' attitudes toward Rayburn had not yet crystallized. Since it appeared that some real issues of the convention were about to be

Schematic presentation of network emphases during seating fight.

ABC	NBC	CBS
1. THE RAYBURN RULING (4:56–7:30 P.M.)		
Video carries the story, but commentary provides first clue to subsequent differences.		
Drama: Orville Freeman, "This is democracy in action."	*Personalities:* Rayburn "confused"; a row has started (as the camera misses initial motion).	*Political strategy:* Orville Freeman will make a floor fight on loyalty pledge.
2. APPEAL OF RAYBURN RULING (7:30–7:50 P.M.)		
Differences among networks emerge.		
Video carries story. Commentary stays out of "drama."	Confusion. Commentator takes role of the viewer.	Commentary identifies floor leaders and their position on seating issue.
3. ROLL CALL ON SEATING VIRGINIA (7:30–9:55 P.M.)		
(a) Expectations begin to structure interpretations.		
Principled fight over ruling to seat Virginia.	Is Rayburn fair? Fight over Rayburn ruling on seating Virginia.	Strategy of coalitions between backers of major candidates.
(b) Illinois switch (8:39) holds key to understanding on all networks.		
North vs. South (8:41–8:45).	"Hidden pressures" and "peculiar rulings," etc. (8:55).	Stevenson forces support seating, but he disavows complicity (9:19).
(c) Linkage supplied by commentary.		
Quick flashes, no general commentary.	Commentary governed by video coverage of floor.	Commentary is linkage between floor coverage and unseen context.

(continued on next page)

ABC	NBC	CBS
4. NOMINATION ROLL CALL RESUMED (9:55–11:45 P.M.)		
Overtones in commentary give individual color to broadly similar context.		
"Hot news" of Stevenson disavowal of complicity (10:25). Resentment at Arvey-Byrd deal and at Rayburn's tactics. Harriman-Kefauver will try for adjournment, which Rayburn will overrule.	Ill will of "liberals" vs. "Dixiecrats" and "bossism." Recess is move against Stevenson and bossism; Stevenson disavowal (10:40). Senator Humphrey will demand roll call to offset gallery shouting.	Convention leadership expects to finish two ballots tonight. Opposition concedes them strength to do so. "So-called liberal coalition" needs time and will use adjournment move as a "test vote" of strength.
5. THE ADJOURNMENT ISSUE (11:45 P.M.–1:07 A.M.)		
Prior context determines ultimate interpretations.		
(a) Douglas calls for adjournment.		
Clash now open.	Senator Douglas and "liberal" backers fight "pressures."	"Kefauver-Harriman liberal coalition" moves to adjourn.
(b) Meaning of vote on adjournment.		
Anti-adjournment votes are mostly from South or for Stevenson.	"Go home" vs. stay and get more accomplished.	Vote to adjourn for Harriman or Kefauver, vote to stay for Stevenson.
(c) Overall interpretation.		
Changes in fortunes are indicative of some big (Stevenson-South) "deal" taking place "behind the scenes."	Focus on confusion and emotions on floor suggests arbitrariness of rulings in interest of South and bosses.	Political strategy called for a test vote of strength on the move to adjourn.

tackled, expectations were high and attention still centered on the delegations and on the impending fracas. Sinister motives were not yet imputed to either side, and the struggle was among political groups with conflicting aims, among whom Rayburn was trying to mediate.

Networks: Orville Freeman, chairman of the Minnesota delegation, immediately rose to protest Virginia's parliamentary inquiry. ABC did no more than identify the person rising. All other ABC comment was restricted to "This is democracy in action." CBS, even before Freeman spoke, indicated his intention to "make the loyalty-pledge business a floor fight." In contrast, NBC, having cut away from routine floor proceedings for a regular news program, inadvertently missed the beginning of the action. Brought abruptly to the convention floor in the midst of what appeared as an uproar, the NBC viewer's only orientation was this brief introduction:

> Rayburn is confused. A row has started. Minnesota and Michigan won't let Rayburn make the rules.

Yet there is reflected in these initial introductions the fundamental outlook of each network. From the outset, the viewer of ABC was led to the *dramatic,* the NBC viewer to the *personal,* and the CBS viewer to the *political* content of any developments. The action centered on Rayburn during this initial phase, and there were frequent close-ups of him on the screen, so interpretations of his facial expressions in line with the "tone" set by each network were soon suggested to viewers.

A second influence on content was the failure of NBC to depict the beginning of the episode. The confusion resulting from the late start, and the lack of a complete fill-in, was compounded by the commentator's insistence that he shared the viewer's confusion.

2. (7:30–7:50 P.M.) *Appeal of Rayburn ruling from floor.* After Rayburn's ruling, the calling of the roll of states for nominations continued. When Maryland was called, Sasscer moved to seat Virginia and thus override Rayburn's ruling. Rayburn, in turn, ruled the Sasscer motion out of order, but this was immediately appealed and a roll call demanded on the appeal.

Networks: During this twenty-minute period, particular differences in the emphases of the three networks began to emerge. ABC let the "action speak for itself" by having the pool cameras and microphones bring it into focus. The CBS commentators, on the other hand, interjected constant pointers about the roles and positions of various floor leaders shown on the screen, who, unmentioned, might have escaped notice. Meanwhile, NBC stuck to easily identifiable, personal content, referring repeatedly to Rayburn and the confusion of the moment. For example:

> Really getting involved now. . . . It'd take a couple of Philadelphia lawyers to straighten this out now. . . . Rayburn getting assistance again [he was consulting with Cannon, the parliamentarian]. . . . big problem now. How does anyone know who is a delegate or not?

> [during a standing vote on a demand for a roll call]. . . . so many interpretations and motions and points of inquiry now that it's a little difficult to keep them all straightened out. . . .

Monitors: The differences in what was accentuated may appear trivial, but resulting differences in viewer orientation can be documented from the notations made by monitors. As the pool camera lingered over a "huddle" in the New York delegation, those watching NBC saw the delegates "arguing" and contributing to the general confusion. CBS monitors perceived the huddle as a "conference" of floor leaders formulating some undetermined strategy (the nature of which they tried to surmise); in other words, it was interpreted as part of the overall contest. Monitors covering ABC evidently failed to take any "cue" whatsoever from this huddle, for in their attempt to understand the fast-moving proceedings they focused almost exclusively on Rayburn and other convention officials.

In the same way, the standing vote and the uproar that followed the demand for a roll call served to confirm, in the absence of clarification, the picture of confusion previously conveyed on ABC, while Rayburn's temporary hesitation in ruling on the roll call conveyed a personal image of a man taken aback by what appeared incomprehensible. The NBC commentator, taking the role of his audience, explicitly shared the personal bewilderment of the soft-spoken Rayburn with them. He suggested no adequate basis for the subsequent ruling to allow the roll call; no cues were conveyed, so that the decision could only appear arbitrary. But for our CBS viewers the uproar was packed with political significance. Since they could identify the contenders, the picture helped to provide them, even in the absence of specific network interpretations, with indications about possible partisan considerations prompting this particular contest. They scanned the action and the actors for hints about the ultimate alignment in the nominating ballot.

3. (7:30–9:55 P.M.) *The roll call on seating Virginia.* The roll call from its outset was interrupted by inquiries about the motion, by temporary passing, by drawn-out polls of delegations. During its second hour, when defeat of the motion to seat Virginia seemed almost certain, numerous switches turned the "no" majorities into majorities in favor of seating.

Context of expectations: The expectations and sensitivities built up during the preceding episodes tended to structure the meaning attributed to the voting. ABC and NBC had emphasized Rayburn's personal and official role in the convention and, as a consequence, unwittingly defined the dispute as a principled fight over his ruling. But the CBS commentary, by supplying basic information about the parties to the dispute, had moved questions of political strategy into focus. Thus, a rumor concerning a pending Kefauver-Harriman coalition was reported equivalently on all three networks. Yet only CBS monitors, their sensitivities sharpened to such clues, were able to connect this information with the floor proceedings. The CBS monitors—but none of the others

—took the vote of Tennessee, the only Southern state solidly against seating, as a clear test for the existence of such a Kefauver-Harriman coalition, even without guidance from the CBS commentary.

The switch (8:39) in the Illinois vote (initially 45 to 15 against seating, then 52 to 8 in favor) signaled, according to all three networks, a significant change in fortune. At this point it became apparent that more was going on than met the camera eye, and all networks ultimately developed a very definite interpretation of just "what was going on."

Network interpretations: Until the general switch of votes became apparent, ABC had explained the vote four times as "determining the seating of Virginia." More detailed political interpretation at that point alluded to the contest as North vs. South. For instance, spotting Jim Farley at 8:41 (two minutes after Illinois' change), an ABC commentator explained:

> I imagine the confusion and division in this convention hurt Jim [Farley] very severely. . . . Yes, that's Jimmy Byrnes. He's perhaps masterminding the whole affair. It was to anticipate the possibility of a Southern revolt led by Byrnes that's caused the North to act as it did.

A few minutes later, at 8:46, it was considered

> . . . very interesting how many states not connected with the South . . . Midwest, Indiana, Illinois—where there is considerable Southern influence—are going with Virginia. Considerable *whispering and conferring*—you see Missouri, a border state, evenly divided.

NBC repeatedly (six times) stressed the confusion, attributing it to delegates' not knowing what they were voting for or to such specific causes as the unit rule and half votes. Or it was simply called "general confusion." The significance of the vote was explained *only* in terms of seating Virginia. Not until some sixteen minutes after the Illinois switch did NBC begin to emphasize "possible pressures on delegates to switch their votes" in favor of the seating. There were no fewer than thirteen references to such, by inference, hidden forces: "pressure from somewhere"; "peculiar rulings that have been made"; "lots of persuasion used apparently"; and so forth.

The interpretation on CBS was limited, until 9:19, to a reportage of voting procedures, to indications of the trend in favor of passage or defeat, and to two references to the "party unity" which was at stake. From 9:19 on, the CBS commentary concentrated on explaining (by collating reports from various sources) the reason for the switching:

> [We're going to] try and make some sense out of what's been happening the last few hours on the floor. . . . The Illinois group . . . changed . . . and we're told at the suggestion of Jacob Arvey. . . . The Illinois move is interpreted as a tip that the Stevenson forces—at least the floor managers for him right now—want Maryland's motion upheld. . . . Stevenson issued a statement that if he [Arvey] did that, he did it without the governor's permission.

According to CBS, Francis Myers, the Stevenson floor manager, had explained that he had been working for the switch because the electoral votes of the South would be very important in the coming election. Other V.I.P.'s in the party were mentioned as helping in the effort to seat Virginia. Interviewed by a CBS reporter on the convention floor, Senator Anderson took credit for having encouraged Senator Russell Long of Louisiana, who had personally complied in signing the loyalty pledge, to cast the entire vote of his delegation in favor of seating Virginia.

The ambiguity of the contest was particularly well suited to bring out differences in the networks' presentation. The underlying issue could be seen as liberal resentment against the more conservative South; or resentment by supporters of the loyalty pledge against a supposedly arbitrary ruling by Rayburn; or an effort to assure Democratic electoral votes in the South; or a test vote by forces behind particular candidates to seat or unseat a delegation whose votes might matter.

Linkages: By examining how the ambiguity of the floor contest was resolved, we can see how the structure peculiar to each style of coverage emerged. Thus, CBS relied on the political acumen of its viewers and, wherever possible, tried to supply politically relevant information. The viewer was thus encouraged to see this as a political contest, and the interpretations of CBS viewers reflected this emphasis. Every event was endowed with a meaning which, in principle at least, was accessible. Where political guidance was lacking, as on ABC, the unfolding convention plot appeared merely as an attempt to bring order out of chaos. Because the workings of the convention were "mysterious" to ABC viewers, the forces at work seemed sinister and clandestine. In the face of quick but unintegrated news flashes by various ABC reporters, the puzzle took on the semblance of an evolving mystery. The only continuing interpretation referred to a North-South contest.

The contrast in content between CBS and ABC is reflected in the definitions by our monitors. A monitor on ABC saw all the switching after the Illinois vote in terms of Rayburn's efforts to placate the South. Rayburn's straightforward inquiry as to whether any other delegation wished to change its vote (8:48) elicited these comments:

> Rayburn *obviously* extending the roll call to placate the South. He is very anxious about this. Very little fill-in [by commentator] about Rayburn's obvious attempt to keep the three states in [some thirteen minutes later].

Whereas on ABC these notions about sinister activities were simply inferred from the lack of explanation and the quick shift of fortunes, the NBC commentator deliberately shared the viewer's imputation of dark forces behind the confused events. Referring to Rayburn, the NBC commentator said:

> Every time someone requests a poll they can't find Sam Rayburn. . . . He has other things on his mind. [Rayburn

had walked off the platform moments before and re-turned immediately after this commentator's remark.]

Some attention was also given to Farley "talking and arguing to beat the band" about an unidentified subject matter.

When, after the Illinois switch, NBC began to talk of pressures and persuasions, the fact that the Illinois chair-man, Jacob Arvey, was known to be a leading Stevenson proponent implied an unholy alliance between his group and the Southern old guard. Any huddles caught by the camera were repeatedly taken as a sign that some-thing was afoot, something that was not quite cricket, a meaning that was indeed absorbed by the NBC monitors.

Another crucial factor in the emergence of divergent definitions was the timing of certain interpretations. Thus, on NBC the idea of a Stevenson-South deal went unrefuted for some hours after the Illinois switch. On CBS, news of the Stevenson disavowal of complicity in the switch was reported while balloting was still in progress. It therefore helped shape partisan definitions of the switch. Both ABC and NBC announced the Ste-venson disavowal only some time after the balloting had ended and the issue was resolved—at least temporarily. Moreover, during the next episode ABC followed the news of the Stevenson disavowal with a report of how Arvey, "the boss of Chicago," had made a deal "on behalf of Governor Stevenson to keep the South in, and they, in turn, are supposed to vote for Stevenson later in this convention." The impact of the ABC and NBC reports of the Stevenson disavowal was lost, and the Illinois switch left the impression of an engineered attempt to force through some "unity" candidate.

4. (9:55–11:45 P.M.) *Nominations roll call resumed.* The nominations roll call and the routine demonstrations for favorite-son candidates were resumed after this interruption of some three hours, during which the convention successfully appealed the chair's ruling not to seat Virginia. All three channels used this resumption of the nominating roll call to analyze previous incidents and to bring the viewer up to date on plans for an adjournment move, which each network anticipated about an hour before it occurred.

Networks: There were no apparent differences in the information offered by the networks. Nonetheless, the preconceptions on which each network developed its own coverage are clear.

ABC may have failed to analyze the maneuvering and switching of votes during the Virginia roll call, but it explicitly related all this to a "deal" within a half hour after the result in favor of seating the non-compliant delegates had been announced. The commentary coupled delegates' resentment at a "so-called Arvey-Byrd" deal with resentment at Rayburn because he had "not counted votes fairly but gaveled through certain proposals." ABC's first anticipation of the move to adjourn (10:45–10:49) was fitted into this context. Resentful Harriman-Kefauver forces were said to be trying for adjournment on this premise:

> They claim there is so much confusion. It is only fair to give them a chance to talk things over. I predict Rayburn will overrule it [the motion to adjourn] and the session will go on all night.

Later, ABC reported a strategy conference called by a group of self-styled liberals and addressed by Hubert Humphrey of Minnesota; these "Liberal-Kefauver forces" (as Humphrey referred to them) were going to call for an adjournment until twelve noon because they needed time to rally their forces. "Watch," said the commentator, "for the strategy to develop on your screen." Directly following this report, ABC interviewed McKinney, chairman of the Democratic National Committee, on the plans for the rest of the evening. Said McKinney:

> . . . a move on foot to recess . . . is to the interest of a particular candidate, not to the interest of the convention. [We're not] going to recess. . . .

The NBC treatment of the interim period was quite similar, except that the continuous talk about "hidden pressures" did not disclose their nature and origin; these continued to be left to the viewer's imagination. Two hours after the vote change, the viewer was told only that ill will had been engendered by the *"mysterious* shift of the Illinois delegation." This "ill will" was borne by "liberals" and directed against "Dixiecrats" and "bossism" (rather than being related to a North-

South fight or Kefauver-Harriman strategy, as on ABC). NBC quoted several delegates to the effect that Rayburn's ruling on Louisiana was part of bossism and a deal with the Dixiecrats. Of the backstage strategy meeting, NBC first told its listeners:

> . . . [the] effort to get a recess . . . of short duration for caucuses . . . [is] to burst the Stevenson balloon . . . and also to burst this control that the liberals are claiming that the bossism people have taken over here at the convention.

Later, Humphrey, in a televised interview, was asked, "Why are you planning this adjournment move?"

> . . . we need the adjournment . . . has been emotion and tension . . . terribly wrong to drive through any kind of final vote on our nominee tonight. . . . We'll use a roll call because I want the delegates in this convention to run the convention. I love the galleries and all the fine people who are working on the floor of the convention, but . . . on a voice vote you have people joining in just because they like to shout.

Meanwhile, CBS continued to emphasize the political strategy involved. It reported that the "leadership" expected to go ahead with the balloting after nominations had been completed. Mike Mansfield of Montana, presiding at the time (11:28), was reported to have said that the convention would go through two ballots. Senator Blair Moody of Michigan, an acknowledged leader in the move to stop the seating of Virginia, had remarked "grimly" to a CBS reporter "that it looks as if they will continue balloting tonight."

The strategy meeting of what it referred to as the "so-called liberal coalition" was placed by CBS within this same context of candidates' chances. Its leaders were said to be determined to keep the convention from going ahead to a ballot. Humphrey had said, "We need time to regroup our forces . . . will use this as a *test vote of strength*." The significance of such a move was clearly noted by a CBS commentator upon hearing this intention:

> If it becomes part of the tactics of the Stevenson and liberal bloc forces to take different sides, it might well be a simple *test vote of strength* to adjourn. That might be one for the books.

Summarizing the contrast in commentary: ABC now explicitly saw the move to adjourn in terms of Kefauver's *political* fortunes and the need to rally forces, rather than as a North-South contest. It was predicted that Rayburn, a Southerner from Texas, whose "fairness" had already become a major issue for ABC monitors, would simply rule the move to adjourn out of order. The viewer was invited to watch the drama unfold. NBC, in line with its policy of supplying a minimum of interpretation, relied largely on Humphrey to clarify the intended move and, through him, thus further paid tribute to "pressures." On CBS the contest was clearly between the convention leadership who opposed adjournment at this time and the "so-called liberal coalition" determined to use, if necessary, a roll call for adjournment as a test vote of its (and, by implication, its opponents') strength.

5. (11:45 P.M.–1:07 A.M.) *The adjournment issue.* As the chairman recognized Governor Battle of Virginia just fifteen minutes before midnight, Senator Douglas could be seen waving a banner and shouting with the support of others, "Mr. Chairman!" Douglas, in an aside, could be heard to remark, "I seem to be having some difficulty although they're looking me straight in the face." Douglas led his associates in continued shouting, disrupting the other business, and repeatedly asked whether the chair would recognize his motion to adjourn. Rayburn, calling a motion to table, did after some ado grant a request from Senator Lehman of New York for a roll call on the tabling of the motion to adjourn. The roll call itself was drawn out by repeated polls of large delegations designed to stall the proceedings, by attempts to challenge the legality of Rayburn's rulings, and by a number of minor wrangles. At the end of the vote, it was evident that the strategy of the Kefauver-Harriman group to force an adjournment and so prevent the convention from going on that night to a ballot for the nomination had failed.

Networks: Each network commented in its own characteristic way on the angry outburst of Douglas to get recognition from the chair. Having anticipated the adjournment move, ABC gave no further explanation of the strategy involved. Pointing to Douglas trying to get Rayburn's attention, the commentator said, *"You know why*. They want to ask for a recess. . . . Since you folks at home know what is going on *behind the scenes*, you know the conflict now is between Senator Douglas and the chairman." Twice thereafter ABC reminded its audience that the recess had been asked for by the "Kefauver-Harriman forces" who needed time for some "fence-mending." In line with its emphasis on "exclusives" and its search for the "inside dope" about the convention, ABC also made three references, while the voting was in progress, to some "big deal." After a vote change by Kentucky on the motion to table, the viewer was told, "When something happens that we don't see or hear about . . . you can count on it that something must have happened." Later this was elaborated as the probability that a deal between the South and Stevenson backers might be shaping up. At the beginning of the vote the opponents of the adjournment had not been identified, but later it was made clear that they were mostly from the South or Stevenson backers.

On NBC the emphasis was on the "liberal" backers of Douglas. The context had previously been supplied: the Douglas-Liberal group needed time to fight certain "pressures" working to advance the Stevenson candidacy. After midnight the viewer on NBC received no guidance as to the purpose of the move. The issue was presented simply as one between those who wanted "to go home" and those who wanted "to stay and get more accomplished." As before, the commentator pronounced himself overwhelmed by the confusion. He continued to read "human emotions" and motives into facial expressions of key figures, but beyond the human drama, no significance was imputed to the progressing roll call.

CBS emphasized the Kefauver-Harriman tactics throughout, most often designating the group as the "Kefauver-Harriman-Liberal coalition," for which Douglas happened to be the spokesman. The commentary on this network had a simple theme: "A vote to adjourn is a vote for Harriman-Kefauver; a vote against is for Stevenson." It described the complexion of the political coalitions and their motives much as did the other networks, but the idea of a *test vote of strength* among the leading candidates was unique to CBS. It limited itself to factual fill-ins. After Douglas had shouted to protest, CBS explained that "the chair has refused to recognize Senator Douglas." During the vote, the "yes" people (in favor of tabling the motion to adjourn) were pointed out as generally for Russell or Stevenson, but such information was not interpreted for the viewer. Nor were there any references to a "deal." Yet the idea of a test vote of strength de-emphasized political and moral issues and focused attention on the tactics employed by each side and their chances for success.

Monitors: CBS monitors, in a final evaluation of the adjournment move, called it a tactical maneuver by the Northern "liberals" who had behaved very badly and forced Rayburn to act as he did. The NBC monitors were furious at Rayburn and felt that they "had never seen anything like that." In part they echoed the commentary, though they had repeatedly discounted it as "stupid." Some examples of their "on-the-spot" interpretations:

> Is this a Rayburn move to keep the party all sewed up tight?
>
> Is Rayburn in cahoots with someone . . . ?
>
> Here it seems impossible to tell how many were for and against. When asked about vote on roll call, says there were not one-fifth of delegates, but it looked like many more.

This emphasis led pro-Stevenson monitors on NBC to favor the adjournment move as a justified "protest" against Rayburn's actions.

ABC monitors, like those on NBC, also focused on Rayburn. One summarized the epilogue during which Louisiana and South Carolina were seated:

> The Byrnes-Stevenson coalition is satisfied since Byrnes will support Stevenson, a moderate civil-righter. So "unity" wins out! The candidate will satisfy the majority of this coalition party.

The North-South axis of the struggle and the hint of "inside dope" on ABC led this pro-Stevenson monitor to condemn that candidate—temporarily.

The inferential structure. Some of our monitors were most critical, to the point of annoyance, at the commentary. Nevertheless, they tended to accept interpretations that were not in line with what they would have wished to believe. Such a finding has an obvious bearing on any evaluation of the role of television in forming political opinion. It caused us even greater consternation when we found, from systematic content analysis, that essentially the *same range of meanings* and the *same factual information* had been available to viewers on each of the networks. The only theme exclusive to one channel was the CBS view of the adjournment move as a "test vote of strength" and its refraining from alluding to any "deals." The overwhelming similarity of manifest content led us to look for more subtle ways in which commentary could generate a conception of the convention that permeated its entire coverage. The coverage, judged by usual indicators, was not "biased." Still, when the same elements were combined into different configurations, viewers on the different networks might draw different inferences, without this being in any way the intent of the network. We have labeled this kind of configuration the *inferential structure* of the telecast.

In the case of the seating dispute and the adjournment move, this inferential structuring of the telecasts resulted in some rather striking forms of unwitting bias. Such structuring influences the way a televised public event comes to be defined. This comes about through network decisions concerning what information is salient at any given moment and through the choice of themes to depict the mood of the convention. The selection of what to show (floor proceedings or background and personalities), the dissemination of background information and interpretation, its timing, the linking of different events to one another are governed by a judgment of what will appeal to audiences. Yet they may at the same time leave an imprint on how the event is transmitted.

Here are some thumbnail sketches of the different styles of coverage of the Democratic convention and how they affected interpretations.

ABC, limited by its smaller staff and unable to compete with the other networks in terms of gadgetry, tried to win audience attention by emphasizing action, wherever it might occur. Thus, it supplied a paucity of information during high points, relying on the picture and sounds of floor activity to hold the viewer's interest. But when the convention proceedings appeared to bog down, ABC tried to maintain the drama by shifting to stories and special features dug up by its newsmen. Frequent shifts of focus may have increased the suspense felt by the audience, but this was often at the cost of an integrated interpretation. Thus, unexplained picture material which did not lend itself to a ready interpretation, and therefore compounded any confusion the viewer may have experienced from frequent shifts of focus, made him more disposed, as during the episodes just discussed, to accept explanations of mystifying turns in terms of "behind-the-scenes" and "kingmaking" activities.

To the extent that ABC emphasized the "action" of the convention, the central figure during the action on Thursday night was Chairman Sam Rayburn. Whatever and whoever was shown on the screen, he was a constant landmark. Given no guidance by the commentator during the early part of the evening, monitors centered their attention on Rayburn and ignored some of the other key figures. As the picture of the floor communicated to the viewer was one of confusion, Rayburn's rulings began to appear as personal arbitrariness, and by the time background and interpretations were supplied, the viewer had been so completely oriented by references to the "unavoidable North-South conflict," the "puzzling Illinois switch," and "backroom strategy" that they were fitted into his picture of sinister forces at work outside the range of the TV cameras.

The principal NBC commentator steered clear of lengthy political analysis. In fact, he interpreted events for his audience while referring to himself as "sitting in a twenty-foot cubicle, watching the same picture as you are." Repeatedly he expressed his bewilderment at what was going on, marveling at Rayburn's "quick decisions" and his "ability to count" the number of voice votes and standees. By this personalization of politics through the use of human-interest angles, he tended to transform tactical maneuvers among the contending factions into issues of faith and distrust of the leading personalities, in this case of Sam Rayburn. Yet Rayburn's actions were not entirely comprehensible to the uninitiated. Seen in personal terms, Rayburn's heavy-handed denial of a request for adjournment appeared as arbitrary.

Hence, Rayburn's personal motives came gradually to be interpreted in the light of the commentator's repeated references to unseen pressures and accumulating ill will. These pressures, whose nature was never identified, were similar to the notion by which the monitors of ABC, unaided by explanations, interpreted their way through the various episodes, except that NBC monitors had the assurance that the network commentator "shared" with them both their image and their confusion.

CBS sought to cover the convention as a news service would. Information was channeled through a central point where various reports were collated and, if used, their source was identified for the viewer. Throughout the long evening, CBS never let its viewers forget the political implications of the many moves on the floor. It attempted to identify each maneuver and with an occasional fill-in tried to "make some sense" of what was being shown. In this way it disseminated the idea that every development had some explanation. As a consequence, viewers saw more and were better able to exercise their own judgments. The incidents appeared to monitors to occur in a much more rational—albeit political—atmosphere, and they interpreted what they saw accordingly, namely as a showdown among several factions with Rayburn trying to mediate.

Truman's Hidden Hand

Many viewers saw Harry S. Truman as kingmaker of the 1952 Democratic convention. In explaining what happened in the course of that convention, 64 per cent of our respondents spontaneously cited him as one of the powerful politicos there. All in all, he received nearly three times as many mentions as either one of his nearest competitors, a competition that put Franklin D. Roosevelt, Jr., in the company of Chicago's Jake Arvey. Senator Douglas, incidentally, was hardly mentioned as a wielder of influence. Neither were most of the actual floor managers, irrespective of how much their activities had been shown over television.

Truman's dominance, according to these same viewers, was exercised through his ability to "influence the voting" and through his "deals" with delegates and candidates alike. What stands out in this connection is the fact that the origin of 40 per cent of the definitions of Truman as a power-behind-the-throne could be traced to other than TV sources; that is to say, as "proof" for Truman's power and influence at the convention, viewers usually cited things read in newspapers, hearsay, or just vague feelings they could not specify, rather than information specifically from the telecast.

That ideas about Truman's influence came from sources other than the convention telecast is in itself not difficult to understand. As President and titular head of the Democratic party, he had been prominent in the news. He had also received his share of abuse as a politician. Apparently his role had already been structured by definitions viewers had of him before the convention. Yet, when viewers did cite evidence from the telecast, they usually referred not to something they had seen but to what they imagined to have gone on in the interim between the close of the day and the beginning of the evening session telecast on Friday, when the convention recessed after the second ballot for the presidential nomination. On the second ballot both Stevenson and Kefauver had amassed new strength. While Kefauver, with 362½ votes, was still ahead of Stevenson, with 324½, no clear-cut decision, no decisive break in the convention appeared in the making. But during that recess Truman arrived in the vicinity of the Amphitheater, and as the convention reconvened, it became clear that Stevenson would win. Viewers referred to whatever had happened during the "gap" in the telecast as evidence that Truman was the kingmaker and that the "draft" of Stevenson was phony.

A detailed examination of the television treatment of Truman's arrival in Chicago and of commentary just before and immediately after the recess indicates how the telecast reinforced any inclination to think of Truman as kingmaker determining the outcome of the convention in a smoke-filled room. This linkage of Stevenson to Truman became a theme in the Republican campaign which followed.

To begin with, Truman's arrival in Chicago while balloting was in progress was treated as a major political event. Both NBC and CBS showed Truman as he was boarding his plane in Washington, while at the very moment the audio carried the vote his alternate was casting for Stevenson as the Missouri delegation was being polled. He arrived near the convention while the second ballot was still in progress. TV viewers had visual proof of his arrival; his presence became superimposed on the temporary deadlock.

Developments between the end of the second ballot (and the afternoon telecast) and the reconvening of the delegates for a third ballot became defined in relation to the visual prominence of Truman. In this way, his personal influence in swinging votes or closing deals could easily be exaggerated. Yet, once suggested, his "unseen" influence could only be considered "backroom activity." Such activities were believed to have led Averell Harriman and Governor Dever (favorite-son candidate from Massachusetts) to withdraw their candidacies and release their delegates as soon as the convention reopened. Immediately the vote on the third ballot began to go Stevenson's way. The "gap" served principally to justify the belief in the "hidden hand" of Truman, exercised from behind the scenes at Chicago. His role was highlighted by a number of elements in the television perspective:

(a) the fact that television did *not* (and could not) cover developments during the recess between the second and third ballots;

(b) the certainty with which many commentators predicted a Stevenson victory even before the *first* ballot had begun during the day session;

(c) the commentators' subsequent puzzlement over the "deadlock" at the end of the second ballot, a puzzlement which was expressly conveyed to the viewer immediately before the "gap," immediately after the "gap," and up to the very moment of Harriman's withdrawal;

(d) the fact that the Harriman switch seemed to have been as much of a surprise to some commentators as it was to some viewers who had counted on a permanent Harriman-Kefauver coalition;

(e) camera and commentator emphasis on the Truman arrival in Chicago and in the vicinity of the convention hall;

(f) TV news coverage of the "gap," recalled by some viewers as a diner-by-diner account of Truman's politicking in a private dining room of the "smoke-filled" Stockyards Inn;

(g) the failure of most commentators to provide any alternative explanations of the "slow changes" during the first and second ballots (for instance, jockeying for the vice presidency), thus underlining what appeared to some as the quick "it's all over but the shouting" change which ushered in the third ballot after the "gap."

We have no documentary evidence of coverage during the "gap," but we can indicate how the commentary contributed to a particular interpretation of what went on between the second and third ballot and to the interpretation, one might say, of "what was not televised." This can be done by contrasting the major themes in the commentary directly preceding and following the recess to alternative explanations of what happened during the interim provided by another medium of mass communication, the magazine.

Before and after the recess: commentators.[7]

ABC

(before gap)

4:09 Kefauver says he will get Harriman's and Dever's votes.

4:50 [watching Truman motorcade] Truman expects to introduce Stevenson tonight.

6:02 Floor leaders for Stevenson predicting victory on fourth ballot.

(after gap)

8:33 Commentator says he [that is, the commentator] had "egg on his face." He went out on a limb, predicted Stevenson would win on first ballot. Russell has no more places to go for votes. Kefauver also has few places to go.

8:37 Can't believe Truman would travel to South Side [that is, to vicinity of convention hall] just for the ride. He intends to give the Stevenson boom and draft a political shot in the arm.

8:40 Truman is eating dinner in the Stockyards Inn. Truman will probably drop hints to Harriman and some Barkley supporters.

(after Harriman statement of withdrawal)

9:17 Truman thinks Stevenson will win on first ballot [that is, third ballot]. Stevenson invited to dine with Truman but did not accept.

7. These are capsule reports of what the commentators said, taken by monitors from audio tapes.

NBC

(before gap)

6:08 Kefauver *and* Harriman have done pretty well so far to offset the Stevenson bandwagon.

6:19 Watch for actions of Southern delegations in next ballot. It may mean a deal for the vice presidency.

6:20 [watching floor] Lots of huddles going on down there. There's going to be a lot of strategy.

6:20 The recess is the most strategic point coming up. May be deals between Stevenson and Russell, Kefauver and Harriman.

(after gap)

8:35 Stevenson is caught in a big squeeze. Stevenson declined an invitation to dine with Truman. . . . Have heard Southern Senators say Stevenson is in. Truman brought along a landslide for Stevenson maybe.

(after Harriman withdrawal)

9:00 Harriman withdrawal a surprise. All comment had been on side of a Kefauver-Harriman combination. Points out that Harriman who started this is the most out-and-out administration supporter, so that this switch was perhaps directed by or certainly approved by Truman.

On CBS, no indication was given before the gap of a possible Kefauver-Harriman coalition. Stevenson was still expected to win, and the voting on the first two ballots was, as noted, interpreted as jockeying for the vice presidency.

(after gap)

8:37 Most experts still think Stevenson will win. Watch for switches in District of Columbia indicating where Harriman votes are going, also Michigan for Kefauver votes. Truman is having dinner at the Stockyards Inn [shown on camera].

8:46 Massachusetts will vote for Stevenson. Predict Stevenson on third ballot.

(after Harriman switch)

8:59 [interview on floor with Lehman and FDR, Jr.] "Stevenson has it on third ballot."

(after Dever statement)

9:03 Importance of fact that liberal candidates are swinging over. Looks like bandwagon rolling for Stevenson.

CBS, unlike the others, did not stress the role of Truman in its *commentary* and provided an alternative explanation to "bossism"—that is, the slow change during the early ballots and the decisions of Harriman and Dever to switch could be attributed to the desire expressed by Humphrey "to save Stevenson for the liberals." There are differences among the commentaries, but whether these in any way overshadowed the determining influence of the "gap," coming as it did in the context of decisive breaks, and in what way the specifics of each commentary contributed to shaping interpretations of Truman's role, we cannot say.

Before and after the gap: press interpretations. Time (August 4, 1952) explained what happened during the "gap" in this way: Truman had "seen" Fitzpatrick, chairman of the New York delegation, and Dever. At the same time, "the facts of life" were brought home to Kefauver. They pointed to a Stevenson victory after the first two ballots and thus led to the rapid change in the pace of events once the convention (and the telecast) resumed:

> Estes Kefauver sat in his grubby bedroom in the Stockyards Inn, a bottle of beer in his hand and a sandwich in his lap. His sleepy eyes were fixed on the TV screen. As he watched the first two ballots, his spirits revived. "I've never been more delighted in my life," said he.
>
> Then James Roosevelt, Governor Mennen ("Soapy") Williams and Senator Blair Moody appeared in the little bedroom to tell Kefauver the facts of life.
>
> He had done better than they expected, but he could never hope to get enough Stevenson or Russell votes for a majority. Truman, who was having dinner on the floor below, had just seen Paul Fitzpatrick of New York and Governor Dever of Massachusetts. Within minutes, Dever would announce his own withdrawal, Fitzpatrick the withdrawal of New York's Harriman. It was all over.

Time's sister magazine, *Life* (August 4, 1952), depreciated Truman's role during the "gap"; the "pros," the "city bosses" had it all set up, and Truman just moved in on the act:

> Though he had been little more than a name to most delegates in Chicago, it had long been obvious that Stevenson would be the party's best candidate. But he was genuinely reluctant, proclaiming that he would an-

> swer only to a genuine draft. So the bosses obligingly forced the draft. This made Mr. Truman's formal announcement of support on the first ballot—by his alternate, Thomas Gavin of Kansas City's first ward . . . purely academic. The party's palace guard had found a strange bedfellow and a strong candidate. . . . The White House moved in on the act.

Richard Rovere, writing in the *New Yorker* (August 2, 1952), discussed at some length how Truman took offense at Stevenson's rejection of his offer of support (January, 1952), then went on:

> Certainly, right up to the moment on Thursday when his alternate, Thomas J. Gavin, announced . . . his vote for Stevenson, President Truman showed Stevenson no more favor than he showed any other man either seeking the office or being discussed as a likely one for the office to seek. . . . For the most part, the White House people, a pretty adept lot when it comes to reading the President's mind and divining his unspoken thoughts, bent their efforts toward the nomination of Barkley. Some of them worked for Harriman. None were prominent in the Stevenson movement.
>
> Thus, it was felt here that the President's decision to have his own vote cast for Stevenson was not reached until after he had become persuaded that Stevenson would win anyway.

Earlier in the article, Rovere stated:

> All during Friday, a fretful day for almost everyone, efforts were made to prevent the Harriman-Kefauver coalition from using its strength to kill off Stevenson;

> equally vigorous efforts were being made to turn the situation to the advantage of Senator Russell or Vice President Barkley. . . . However, the stop-Stevenson movement had already begun to lose its momentum as early as Friday morning, and although it still had followers that afternoon, they were becoming fewer by the hour, their leaders were walking out on them, and President Truman was flying in from Washington to deliver the *coup de grâce to* the whole affair, *whether or not a* coup de grâce *was needed.*

Other weekly magazines, *Newsweek* (August 4) and the *Reporter* (August 19), in their post-convention issues, supported the explanation that it was all over but the shouting by the end of the second ballot, that the only question mark was who was going to put Stevenson across—who was going to start the bandwagon. Thus, each of the five magazines saw Truman hurrying things up during the "gap," although they varied in their descriptions of just how the President went about this. Though they disagreed on who or what was responsible for Stevenson's being "in" by the end of the second ballot, they presented interpretations of what happened during the "gap" which made those activities seem less unfathomable, less "sinister" than the TV perspective.[8]

Given the prior context on TV, the viewer was led to interpret the "gap" as the key to Truman's decisive role at the convention. The gap reinforced any predilec-

8. For an insider's story, see Walter Johnson, *How We Drafted Adlai Stevenson,* New York, Knopf, 1955.

tion to view Truman's part as important and suggested that sinister forces were engaged in hidden maneuvers. And the failure of commentators to provide a sound interpretation of what happened during the recess probably contributed further to this notion.

Conceptions of "Neutrality" and Their Consequences

These three cases from the 1952 nominating conventions document three ways in which television commentary can structure a televised event. The commentary has considerable impact on definitions of complicated and somewhat ambiguous incidents, even when TV reporters typically abrogate to the camera the responsibility for reportorial accuracy.[9] It also helps dramatize the activities of persons who appear on the screen without dramatic emphasis and whose role would otherwise remain obscure. Finally, the commentary helps to structure inevitable gaps left in the video by providing transition and context.

In each case we have discussed, the interpretation promoted seems to have resulted without any deliberate intent on the part of the commentator. Rather, all interpretations seemed to hinge on assumptions made by each network about its audience. How different assumptions lead to different interpretations has been fully

9. See the next chapter.

demonstrated only in the instance of the Democratic seating fight, when we had a quasi-experimental situation in which we could use our monitors to document the differences in styles of reporting. Among our panel of viewers, by contrast, linking any particular interpretation to the telecast involved a considerable degree of inference. Nonetheless, the reactions of our monitors and the reports obtained from our panel tend to substantiate and supplement each other. The data drawn from interview materials, moreover, are in line with other mass communications findings in suggesting (1) that these effects are compounded by a process of self-selection, with each member of the mass audience seeking that network and that commentary most congenial to his basic conception of politics; and (2) that viewer interpretations have a special authenticity, for viewers believe they have "seen for themselves"—they are unaware they have been influenced by the style of coverage.

IV

OPERATION VIDEO: THE LIVE COVERAGE OF EVENTS

No communications network is completely neutral. Any translation of an event into a message inevitably involves screening and interpretation in terms of concepts. The symbolic content, i.e., the concept, through which the essential features of the event are communicated can approximate but not duplicate the reality. Even the live coverage of an event by television, as studies of MacArthur Day and the 1952 nominating conventions convinced us, represents that event from a unique point of view. The exaggerations and distortions that result may not appear very significant—indeed, some newsmen are prone to deny that they exist. When told about some of our convention findings, a producer who had charge of operations for one network responded indignantly, "All we can do is show people what's going on. If they misinterpret it, that's not our responsibility."

This producer's attitude is no longer as representative as it was at the time. Television journalism has become more self-conscious over the years. Being aware that any decision may have unintended consequences certainly offers a better guarantee against bias than seeking cover behind the presumed automatic reportorial accuracy of the camera.

This chapter examines, from the newsman's point of view, the standards and practices that govern the reporting of public events on television and the decisions through which they are implemented. For this purpose, we held interviews with some twenty-odd news managers, reporters, cameramen, and others who had participated in the reporting of the 1952 conventions, using our observations of these telecasts to solicit explanations of practices. Material from these interviews has been supplemented with other accounts by TV newsmen about their experiences in the coverage of public events.

Norms and Standards

Television newsmen consider themselves members of the working press. They accept norms that have been the hallmarks of good journalism everywhere, such as accurate, objective, and balanced reporting which conforms to standards of "good taste." These norms have been incorporated into professional codes, and they receive explicit backing in policy statements of management. In fact, these standards are so much accepted that they require no further elaboration here.

What should be noted, however, is that, despite the powerful opinion-shaping instrument that television newsmen wield, they rarely see themselves functioning as educators. The term hardly occurred in our interviews, but whenever it did, newsmen tended to reject its relevance for themselves. One young television journalist actually warned us in advance, just as we were about to begin our interviewing, that "the important thing in approaching the news staff is never to speak of their job in terms of educational effects. They consider themselves reporters and not educational broadcasters. They look on their job here [at the conventions] as reporting, getting a story, in much the same manner as the members of the working press in any other medium."

The clear identification of the TV newsmen with the working press, rather than with any particular medium, also led them to dissociate themselves in no uncertain terms from those among their colleagues who deliberately deviated from objective reporting. For example, although nearly the entire news staff in those early days of television journalism had been recruited directly from radio, they had little sympathy for some well-known commentators who had achieved notoriety and a personal following through their sensational treatment of the news on that medium or for their highly partisan point of view. One television reporter, who had his own newscast on a local station, minced no words in telling us:

> Some people criticize ——— for what he does. I don't see it that way. If you're running a whorehouse, you may be doing a good job in that capacity. This isn't what these people are doing. Let them. But that isn't the function of a reporter or analyst. Our job is to report the news and its background without trying to compete in any other business.

Evidently, most television newsmen, clearly not in the business of education, do not see it as their function to arouse and agitate the public over matters they believe, individually or collectively, should be its concerns.[1]

Television newsmen insist they are doing the same things as their colleagues in the fourth estate, despite the fact that the format of the newspaper is largely determined by its function as a purveyor of topical news and information, while television has been treated from the very beginning as a medium dedicated primarily to entertainment. A television producer put it this way:

> The job of TV is to get the news, to show what it is like. It is *not* entertainment, nor is it information. TV is

1. The matter becomes more complicated with a national educational television network. The line between reporting and education becomes thinner and may create a change in the newsman's orientation to news.

> something in the nature of a transportation medium. It takes the viewer to the scene of the crime. It is like being there. The viewer is there and sees what it is like. In sports, if I may give you an example, it's like being at the Army-Navy game, to see it alive. . . . We are laying out what is happening as it is happening. We cannot edit. We are restricted to making our coverage and telling the story as it is happening.

To realistically weave together many visual elements into a coherent news story, to bring an event into focus *while* it is happening, is one of the main goals of TV reporting. Most television newsmen think they can do this better than other media, because television adds to the spoken or written word the element of actuality, which is the unique characteristic of the visual dimension.

The power of television lies, in the words of one network vice president, in the "provision of enlightenment through exposure." [2] This alone, presumably, is enough to place the announcer under great constraint. Thus Eric Sevareid, CBS news analyst, once referred in a press interview just before the 1952 convention to television as being "kind of scary. You get a sense of power in television. It's like hanging on to the throttle of a locomotive. Everybody's watching you like a hawk. You mustn't betray the slightest emotion that shouldn't be there. People must get the feeling you're trying to be fair." [3]

2. Cited in C. A. Siepmann, *Television and Education in the United States,* Paris, UNESCO, 1952, p. 45.
3. *New York Times,* July, 1952.

The same point has been made, though perhaps less graphically, by others: If television reporting differs from other reporting, this difference lies in the opportunity to use the technology of the medium as an ally. In the proper use of television, the truth is told *through,* rather than *over,* the medium.

There is a branch of psychology that has addressed itself explicitly to the problem of accuracy in testimony. Its cumulative findings point to a number of possible sources of error in any report. Witnesses often misperceive an event. Particularly when the action is fast-moving and involves many people, their observations often entail basic errors. With the passage of time, the reliability of testimony suffers further decline through memory lapses. Yet, even where observation and recall are highly accurate, distortions can arise from the inability of the witness to express himself accurately in his account of the event.

With the cameras carrying the burden of telling the story, TV reduces this kind of *personal* "bias," even though commentary that is still necessary may well influence what a person "sees." But let us note that this erosion of personal bias in observation, recall, and communication comes from the intervention of a complex machinery, which no individual reporter, no matter how enterprising or skillful, can possibly match through his own resources. The live coverage of an event is something other than a single story pieced together. It is told through an organization that involves collaboration among cameramen, reporters, editors, and producers. In more spectacular efforts, such as covering a convention, an election, or a state funeral, literally hundreds of clerical, technical, and news personnel pool their efforts under the direction of a producer, who deploys their resources, skills, and energies to what he sees as the best advantage.

Given these conditions of production, any bias or slant must be traced to the way these efforts are integrated at every level of the organization. Distortion takes on impersonal overtones because individual lapses and misjudgments can be corrected, and a network will use the resources it has committed to live coverage to check as far as possible on every unconfirmed or questionable report. This does not mean that all initiative and individual judgment are thereby eliminated. On the contrary, reporters still must be alert to possible news breaks and must signal for camera crews in anticipation of developments, and camera crews must close in on a picture with some idea of how it is going to be used. But even here corrections are possible. A commentator who, during a live show, suggests to his audience that "just to the left of the picture you see on the screen—just a little outside of it—something seems to be going on" may in fact be signaling the director or the camera crew to get and transmit the best picture.

Whatever leeway individuals have in using the technology and resources at their command must be exercised within the framework of an overall policy. Consequently, if personalities have an influence on what is disseminated, this occurs largely through their ability to influence the organization through which they operate. In some instances, the unique style characteristic of an organization may reflect the special ability of one person to translate his own vision into a corporate structure. The late Edward R. Murrow had, according to his co-producer, considerable influence on the CBS public affairs coverage and on the standards it set for news reporting.[4] But much policy that governs day-to-day improvisations evolves simply through informal discussion and the haphazard evaluation of past experience. Sometimes the reactions of camera crews and personnel in the monitoring room are accepted as cues for what goes over; the reactions of critics and viewers form another element in evaluation.

Policies and Practices: Variations

Television newsmen, to repeat, think of themselves as reporters getting a story and telling it through their medium. Everyone interviewed expressed his strong commitment to objectivity. There is also much pride, and some humility, about the power imputed to TV, but newsmen emphatically rejected any responsibility for unfavorable—though unintended—effects of the transmission of "actuality."

There are, nevertheless, various means through which to implement the general standard of objectivity (neu-

4. Fred Friendly, *Due to Circumstances Beyond Our Control,* New York, Random House, 1967, *passim.*

trality). One possibility is to take as literally as possible the notion that "the picture speaks for itself." The announcer thus takes a back seat, making the most of the live picture and sound and filling in only when this appears absolutely necessary. A second approach seeks to achieve objectivity and neutrality by exploiting television's potential for the "instant reply." In this view, an opportunity to confirm or refute any ambiguous or controversial report or statement must be offered immediately to those involved or directly affected. "Focus in depth" is a third alternative. Like the first, this involves a basic reliance on "actuality," except that the news staff supplies all the necessary context for an understanding of the events being transmitted.

Differences among these three approaches are primarily differences in emphasis. Though they are not mutually exclusive alternatives, to emphasize one more than the others does influence the character of the coverage.

The picture worth a thousand words. If one views the television coverage of an event as complementary to that of the printed media, the prime contribution of the camera is immediacy, not contextual coverage. Accordingly, television tells the story as it happens, without any editing and with comment on the picture limited to what is absolutely required. Interpretation and context will be provided by the newspaper (or news magazine). Editorials and columnists offer comments and opinion, while news articles provide interested readers with analysis in depth.

Here is how one network executive justified a policy of providing minimal interpretation:

> We are forcing the newspapers more and more into a position where they *have* to give interpretation. . . . Look at the front page of the *New York Times,* for instance, and see how many interpretative articles you see. Before television they used to be straight stories. For example, during the Nixon speech [the famous Checkers speech of the 1952 campaign], we brought it as it happened while the newspapers satisfied the want for interpretation—what it meant, its significance, and other evaluations. People want newspapers to fill in. . . . We tell the running story, whereas the press ties up the story.

Following this practice, commentary by the network was deliberately held to a minimum to let events at the Republican and Democratic conventions tell as much of the story as possible. Commentators were cautioned against doing too much "explaining of the picture." One informant recalled that, on at least one occasion, "We told the announcers to keep quiet to let the picture speak."

This network tried as much as possible to simplify the story of the conventions. It wanted, in particular, "to show the audience that these politicians were just people." This goal was implemented by assigning the anchor man a rather limited function. The network put him in the control room, where he could look at the monitor, and laid down the

> policy that, as a TV commentator, he should not talk about things that are not seen. . . . Our feeling about [this man] was that he really knew politics and the people in it. In our view, the role of a commentator is that of a friendly but knowledgeable man. He is to be the same as a person sitting next to you, watching the set with you. To be sure, he has more knowledge and experience and he supplements the picture, even if it is merely by identifying the figures on the screen.

Along the same line, cutaways for interviews or special commentaries were to be offered only when they would not disturb the continuity of the event and so interfere with the viewer's efforts to think things through for himself. Interpretations in depth were generally relegated to on-air time before individual sessions or, in the case of an episode that clearly acquired amplification, *after* the action had more or less terminated.

> This notion that "the job of TV [was] . . . to stay with the convention as much as possible . . . emerged in the course of covering the first [Republican] convention" without any explicit discussion or final decision. We [the authors] asked whether this policy had been based on any indicators of audience reaction, such as phone calls from viewers. Complaints (as well as praise) of all kinds were received, but this network's policy was "first to let the audience know that the floor was dull before we cut away for something else."

The same kinds of judgments had to be made by the other networks, as the following two quotes illustrate:

After you've seen five minutes of a demonstration,[5] you've seen all of it, and after you've seen a demonstration for Taft or Eisenhower, you've also seen the one for Warren and the other candidates. . . . One is just like the other. . . . During a demonstration we had to ask ourselves whether people wanted to see the demonstration or, for instance, Mrs. Taft, or the Warren demonstration rather than the Warren girls [the daughters of Chief Justice Earl Warren, then governor of California]. We thought people would be more interested in getting the Warren girls' reaction to their father's nomination than seeing the same type of demonstration over again.

When we cut out of the conventions, the audience called. Not only the people whose delegates were about to be polled, but others also preferred to watch the polls. There was apparently a lot of human interest in this, which people wanted to see. Even in the Democratic convention, where it really got drawn out, we kept a good part of the polling on the air.

In 1952, NBC, more than other networks, relied on the camera to tell the story. It became committed to staying with proceedings on the floor, even when they were routine. It provided actuality and emphasized the human-interest side—a style of coverage that continues to characterize its coverage of public events.

The instant reply. Live coverage can approximate

5. That is, the planned "spontaneous" demonstration which followed each nomination for President or Vice President.

something we have called the "instant reply," that is to say, immediate reactions can be elicited from relevant participants by ordering lines to chief points of interest where news stories are likely to break, and by exploiting the mobility of equipment. Participants in events have an opportunity to add to TV's coverage; at the conventions, for example, contenders and their managers could refute rumors, dispute uncontested claims, or evaluate one another's strategies. This certainly adds to the drama of a convention. It also lets the viewer follow developments from a number of angles and, where there is doubt or difference, puts him in a position to judge.

This is how various members of the ABC staff described their orientation:

> We thought of sideshows more often than the others. We were always looking for new angles that hadn't been thought of before. . . .
>
> We thought many times that floor time—straight coverage of the convention floor—was wasted time and we could do better by going behind the scenes. But we did things behind the scenes only if they were newsworthy.
>
> You were always supposed to be looking for a story. Through our five or six reporters, we could cover any point at which a story developed. We worked as a news service. We tried to cover all angles of the convention wherever there was the greatest news interest.

The main point was to get the "jump" on the other

networks. Although—indeed, because—ABC had much less equipment and personnel than the other two networks, it "tried to make more of a show out of the convention, instead of simply allowing it to run its course."

Thus, the decision to make a play for the "sideshows" was deliberate, but ABC did not have many alternatives. It was competing against more established networks, and all its network affiliates were in multichannel communities. Consequently, everywhere it had to draw its audiences away from other stations. Whenever the floor proceedings were dull, it reasoned, or whenever there was a commercial, the viewer would flick the dial to another channel to see what it was showing. Ultimately he would stick with the network that brought him the best show. Thus, ABC styled its coverage, not vis-à-vis the newspaper that could serve as ally, but largely in terms of the networks with which it had to compete.[6]

ABC also gave its commentators considerable prominence. "Our staff of commentators was the best advertised, both with regard to quality and quantity . . . . and we had all sides, all shades of opinion represented. Big names among your commentators are important. We had them. We could, for example, present a commentary by ———— and then balance it with an interpretation from ————." ABC also would balance a

6. Sixteen years later ABC broke with tradition and announced it would not attempt full coverage of the 1968 nominating conventions.

specialist on the human side of the news with a specialist on the science of politics, each giving his own slant. Balance and objectivity were maintained by giving equal exposure to all sides. In some respects the format was similar to that of televised debates (see Chapter VI), where the direct confrontation of two contenders contributes to the drama but there is a rigid enforcement of the equal-time rule.

Focus in depth. Neither maximum exposure with minimal guidance nor a near-simultaneous juxtaposition of divergent viewpoints will assure the clarity of political meanings inherent in a televised event. To present a picture of complicated events in some depth requires a well-organized reporting system. To paraphrase, things are not just what is seen. Only on the basis of available reports can a director decide where to send his cameras and how best to fill in for the viewer. The idea that TV is just the picture was emphatically rejected by a number of newsmen we interviewed as an "untrue shibboleth"—the transmission of actuality requires "proper presentation and interpretation." In fact, one CBS producer said, "You can be no better in your televising than the reporting to the top."

The CBS coverage in 1952 was aimed explicitly at what one of their top producers called:

> a reasonably adequate picture of the whole complex of the convention. We wanted a political coverage of the conventions. . . . We reported seriously and concen-

> trated on the political meanings. We refrained from interviews with purely human-interest appeal—humor and so forth. . . . It's not up to us to make it a good show. It's not a show but a convention. Our job was to let people know and help them to understand what was going on at the convention.

CBS used its commentary to supply the necessary context, though it did not ignore special interviews or live shots of events off the floor. Studied objectivity is required in factual and interpretive commentaries, and the right kind of pictorial material must be available.

No matter how competently and responsibly telecasters put together the significant vignettes that tell the story, presenting the news "in depth" necessarily entails a partial abandonment of the idea of telling the news as it happens. Hence, the public affairs special, a documentary of some length based on film or video tape, has been used in more recent world and domestic crises. Television critics have acclaimed such efforts as responsible coverage, and the combination of vivid picture material and intelligent commentary has produced some stunning examples of what television journalism at its best can do. Television reporting in these specials seems to be moving closer to the weekly news magazine, told with picture materials, with each staff developing its unique style.

Newsmen on these specials still see themselves as reporters in pursuit of hot news, but the documents they help make possible seem more and more to be fulfilling an educational function. We are sure that even those TV newsmen who are educators at heart would deny this most emphatically. Yet the practice, now commonplace, of networks issuing pamphlets on how to view the nominating conventions, on how to follow an election, on how to size up the trends on election night, and so on, though undertaken with an eye toward publicity, nevertheless constitutes a broadening of the journalistic function.

A Good Story

Sometimes the audience is the final determinant of the news it gets and of the quality of reporting. But, on the whole, the kind of reality the media create is the product of a group of communicators whose members are only indirectly in touch with the audience they address. Mass communicators produce for a market rather than for a particular audience. The absence, for all practical purposes, of a direct channel of audience response means that the mass communicators talk considerably more to their audience than they listen, while at the same time they listen more to each other than to their audience. News coverage is shaped more by the standards of the industry and its professionals than by its actual audience and its reactions.

Like their colleagues in other media, TV newsmen are always after a good story. A good story in their medium is one that lends itself to visual presentation and contributes to the viewer's understanding of some important event. All are agreed that significant news should never, under any circumstances, be sacrificed for trivial picture material. To be able to size up on the spur of the moment the news value of an incident is the kind of judgment that journalists pride themselves on having. They usually talk of sound news judgment as a sixth sense acquired only with experience. Newsmen can furnish many specific illustrations but rarely can define it in more general terms.

The coverage of the 1952 conventions had obviously been shaped with an eye toward self-dramatization. Each organization eagerly seized the opportunity to display its newest equipment, initiative, and skill. Members of the various news staffs, understandably, derived considerable satisfaction from their personal participation in the major journalistic achievement of their organization. They talked happily of incidents where they had gotten the jump on the press or on rival networks and pointed to a number of television "firsts."

Competitive considerations affect the nature of all non-pooled public affairs coverage, and the networks keep a continuous watch on one another. In 1952, none of the networks was prepared to cede the field to its rivals lest an unexpected news break occur. Said one respondent, when asked how the decision to give full coverage was taken: "We stayed for such long hours largely because of our competitors. We would watch them and sometimes were wondering whether we should go off, especially during the committee sessions. We would notice that the others were still on. So we stayed, too." In the same way, they also watched one another's format, determined to duplicate the others' successes while avoiding their errors. In 1964, CBS, during the Republican convention, lost the ratings game to NBC mainly due to the popularity of the Huntley-Brinkley team, known for its witty, human-interest treatment of the news. Its answer for the Democratic meetings was to replace its experienced anchor man, Walter Cronkite, with a two-man team, Roger Mudd and Robert Trout, and give its coverage a "light touch" imitation of NBC. Though CBS did improve its ratings, it was also chided for not sticking to its notion that a convention was a convention, not a show. Hal Humphrey of the *Los Angeles Times* wrote that "last week's scuttling of Walter Cronkite . . . put him on the same level as a comic whose jokes weren't registering high enough on the laugh meters." By November, in the CBS coverage of election night (see Chapter VII), Cronkite was back again. The rating battle, however, still went on.

During the 1952 conventions, competition sometimes took the form of gaining entry where others had failed. In an extreme competitive scramble, an operator might end by jarring a rival camera out of focus or by getting between it and the subject making news. Most of the time, however, each network sought to distinguish itself by lining up important individuals for interviews in its studios or, if they were too busy, by buttonholing them on the floor or in the halls and lobbies. One reporter considered it a special achievement that his network had obtained interviews in the "caucus room"; few viewers could ever have seen one from the inside before.

An ABC newsman told how his network, unable to match the others in equipment, had been forced to improvise in covering the story of Vice President Barkley's withdrawal from the race. ABC, he told us, had received an advance tip and consequently dispatched one of its reporters to the Blackstone Hotel. This reporter, when he got there, telephoned his studio to confirm the imminent announcement and to request a camera and crew to cover the story live. But ABC had no available camera to send. However, the reporter was using the only phone available near where Barkley would emerge to meet the press. He was told to hold on to it, and did so for ninety minutes. The viewer of ABC eventually watched the announcer in the studio taking the story of Barkley's withdrawal as the reporter phoned it in. In this way, "We got the first report on Barkley. The press did not get it till one hour later. We had the phone. They were slow because their wires were clogged." Unable to show the event live, ABC nevertheless capitalized on the activities and ingenuity of its own staff.

This anecdote also illustrates the eagerness of newsmen and their organization to give themselves credit for getting to the scene of special events. During the coronation of Queen Elizabeth II, which occurred some years prior to Telstar, the networks went to such lengths to be the first on the air with their newsreels that the outcome of the race itself became a major news event. Whenever a newsman himself becomes a central focus of attention, as in a brush with rioters or with the law, this only adds to the actuality and helps to create news. One of the highlights of the televised 1964 conventions came when an NBC reporter was arrested for not heeding the order of a local policeman to clear the aisles. This reporter was then able to give a blow-by-blow account, in front of the camera, of his own arrest and departure to the police station.

Some incidents which the networks hailed as major accomplishments were really no more than cashing in on accidents. Several of those who had participated in the televising of the 1952 conventions thought one of the high points in electronic journalism was the live pickup of President Truman, waving and smiling as he boarded his plane in Washington to fly to the convention in Chicago, at the precise moment the audio brought in from the Amphitheater the voice of his alternate in the Missouri delegation casting a vote for Stevenson.[7] Similarly, an alert cameraman for one network was able to catch, during the funeral of President Kennedy, a live shot of three-year-old John saluting his father's flag-draped casket. Or a publication of the CBS news staff recalls with special pride that, in 1956,

7. See Chapter III.

"when the cameras sought out Senator Kefauver of Tennessee during a brief stopover at Washington National Airport for comment on his political plans, they got the comment. They also got a priceless picture of Mrs. Kefauver hastily kissing her traveling husband and handing over a box of clean shirts for his next campaign swing." [8] In itself a sidelight that eluded the wire services, the episode was cited as giving the viewer a vivid insight into the hectic nature of a campaigner's life.

Yet to be able to cash in on such accidents presupposes much advance preparation. An account by Perry Wolff illustrates the kind of judgment that must be made on the operating level whenever some major news break is anticipated. In covering his assignment at the Stevenson headquarters in Springfield, Illinois, on election night, 1952, Wolff's most difficult decision was where to place the only three cameras he had. For optimum coverage, it seemed, he could put one camera in a small room for interviews; another could be used in the ballroom of the Leland Hotel, to be kept in readiness for any statement the governor would make; he could then place his third camera outside the executive mansion, where Stevenson would be spending the evening following the returns as they came in. "But if I did this," Wolff wrote, "and if the ballroom camera

8. CBS News, *Television News Reporting,* New York, McGraw-Hill, 1958, p. 84 f.

should fail at the critical moment, I would have no way to transmit the speech. For safety's sake, I should not use the camera at the mansion, but should use it as insurance in the ballroom. While this may seem to the casual reader a minor decision, television producers have been sent back to radio for less. I decided to keep the camera at the mansion and trust to luck. I reasoned that if the Governor won he would make an acceptance speech at every street corner in Springfield, and if he lost I merely would be compounding the tragedy." [9]

These incidents illustrate what has often been defined as the primary problem of live coverage: how best to let the viewer in on the significant moment. At times, television has indeed done this superbly. Yet such results, as we have seen, depend on careful preparation. They do not come automatically but require a constant balancing among considerations.

Choices are somewhat simplified when the event to be covered is highly predictable, as in the case of an official ceremony where primary interest lies in the pageantry. Emergencies resulting from unexpected failures are not thereby excluded, but the way such events are scheduled makes it easier to coordinate the coverage with the event. What takes place becomes so predictable that the placement of cameras, the sequence of shots, and an appropriate commentary can be pre-

9. Perry Wolff, "TV Man at the Stevenson Watch," *Harper's*, CCVI (January, 1956), 66.

pared before hand. Thus, one of the authors was "behind the scenes" during the television premiere of the ceremonial opening of the Canadian parliament in 1955. Highly sensitive to criticism that TV by its mere presence might detract from the solemnity of the event, the public affairs staff of the Canadian Broadcasting Corporation had determined in advance every camera shot and had prepared a written commentary in separate French and English versions. Nothing was left to chance. Nevertheless, the viewer watching the "live" telecast could applaud the smooth and restrained descriptions and not sense in the least that the narrator was simply reading from a prepared script.

The decision on how best to let the gadgets tell their story sometimes leads to a compromise with "actuality." In this regard, the working newsman is not above an occasional bit of deceit in the interest of a "story." Since he is rewarded for obtaining such vignettes, there may be some shelving of objectivity provided the deception can be considered insubstantial and involves no essential distortion.[10] The director of film camera crews at the 1952 conventions expressed great satisfaction about the way they had been able to use their high-speed developer. It had assured them a constant supply of film in short order: "People couldn't know it was

10. In the same way, Warren Breed argues with respect to the staffer on a small-town daily that the focus on "getting more news" as a central value tends to soften policy conflicts concerning objectivity. See "Social Control in the Newsroom: A Functional Analysis," *Social Forces*, XXXIII (May, 1955), 331.

film," he said. "We would announce it at the beginning, but then treat the show as 'live.' Many people, I am sure, were never aware it was film." Another network, hoping to forestall calls from viewers concerned with events on the floor, made a deliberate practice of deleting a third or fourth seconding speech, which it judged to be without political interest, by cutting away *before* the speaker had even begun. As a consequence, it argued, when the viewer returned to the floor for the following speech, he would have no way of knowing he had missed anything.

The question is when this kind of editing, done without destroying the illusion of actuality, ceases to be legitimate. The question assumes special import since television justifies its quest for "equal access," on a par with the other news media, by emphasizing its uncompromising objectivity. In the pre-television age, a public figure, including the President, who granted an interview to members of the press might request the deletion of remarks made off the record, and his request would be granted. For example, for many years it had been established practice that any direct quotation of the President at his news conference required his explicit consent. Under the Eisenhower administration, press conferences were televised not "live" but on film, so they could be pre-edited (censored) before release. By the time Kennedy came to office—and since—press conferences have been televised "live." Public figures less often resort to the privilege of deleting a remark; the effect of such editing has most often been to draw attention to what has been deleted.

Some years ago, John Daly, as the spokesman for ABC, took a stand against this form of censorship on TV. His network had contracted with the Fund for the Republic for a series of extended and free-ranging interviews with public figures, but Daly refused to telecast an interview with Henry Cabot Lodge on the ground that several remarks had been edited out at the latter's request. The gist of his argument was that, to the viewer, the filmed interview had the semblance of actuality and simultaneous relay. For this reason, no tampering with "live" events was permissible, and the film would either have to be shown in its original unedited version or not at all. Under no conditions, Daly argued, should television coverage of this kind be allowed to serve as an adjunct of the public relations staff of any individual or group.

Still, there are limits to unrestricted publicity, and these turn on distinctions between public and private figures. Newsmen implicitly accept the principle that they should not invade anyone's privacy. Our interviews revealed that to make a spectacle out of the personal mannerisms of an innocent bystander, televising him in an unguarded moment, would certainly be a breach of good taste. So would the exposé of, let us say, the ignorance of an amateur. Newsmen feel obligated to exercise self-restraint in protecting private individuals from the prying eye of a roving camera.

Suppression in the name of good taste—or in consideration of libel laws—is one of the duties of the working press.

With public personalities the matter stands quite differently. "They're on their own, and they've got to be on the alert, knowing that the eyes of the public are on them," explained one newsman. If someone should inadvertently let the cat out of the bag or display bad temper when badgered by questions, there would be absolutely nothing improper in showing this on television.

The whole problem is complicated because the line between what is private and what is public about a well-known personality cannot always be distinctly drawn. Serious consideration, wrote members of the CBS news staff, should always be given to discarding film material that "would tend to reflect disfavor on a person whose news position is not in itself controversial or unfavorable." [11] Yet it is not very likely that there would be unanimity on what should be discarded.

The increased use of film and tape, in place of live coverage, raises special considerations, particularly since news-gathering organizations now have large libraries of such materials from which to select highlights or splice together an interpretive documentary. Since such editing is always selective, it puts the question of television's inherent objectivity in a new light. The half-

11. CBS News, *Television News Reporting*, p. 95 f.

hour program Edward R. Murrow did on Senator Joseph McCarthy, broadcast March 9, 1954, was a striking display of what skillful hands and heads can do with such film material. The program was superbly edited from films and tapes of the senator in action. His career was laid out before the public mainly with McCarthy himself telling the story in his own words and pictures —McCarthy laughing at Eisenhower, attacking Stevenson with his "Alger [Hiss], I mean Adlai," badgering witnesses, condemning by innuendo. In deference to the potential power of TV as actuality, Murrow kept himself, for the most part, in the background, except when he offered McCarthy the opportunity to reply on the program if he "believes we have done violence to his words or picture," and in an editorial concluding the half-hour: "This is no time for men who oppose Senator McCarthy's methods to keep silent, or for those who approve."

The program was no doubt an effective television exposé of a controversial figure at a time when he was at the zenith of his national influence. It has since often been cited as the first critical blow to the myth of the senator's invincibility. To the best of our recollection, only two commentators—other than the senator's partisans—addressed themselves to the implications this telecast had for the standards governing television reporting; both critics of McCarthy, they were John Cogley, writing in *Commonweal,* and Gilbert Seldes, writing in the *Saturday Review.*

The issue raised was the use of an impartial documentary program, with all the prestige it enjoyed, for an attack on an individual; the fact that McCarthy himself had used his access to the news media to destroy so many reputations was no excuse for turning the table on him. Did Murrow's offer of "equal time" assure fair treatment? Could the impression created by an attack that had at its disposal the full facilities of a professional organization, the skills of its personnel, and the use of its libraries, ever be undone by the efforts of an individual who, though a public figure, lacked equal facilities? The program showed how the camera, which allegedly depicts actuality and therefore requires no reply, can be used to mount a partisan attack on an individual or cause.

McCarthy did respond on April 6. That answer, Seldes wrote, was "a brilliant demonstration of the fallacy involved" in the formula of equal time. The original broadcast, Seldes pointed out, was "the product of some three years of experience in the handling of film clips, an art in which Murrow and his co-worker Fred Friendly have no peers." McCarthy's reply was "dull," a "feebly handled newsreel talk illustrated by two or three animated maps—about as weak a television program as you could devise." [12]

Political figures, for their part, have tried to master

12. *Saturday Review*, April 24, 1954, pp. 26–27, 37.

what Seldes dubbed the art of the semi-fake.[13] Believing that the most effective political television is spontaneous, yet wary of the perils of "live" performances, slips of the tongue, technical failures, and so forth, they avoid spontaneity but try to appear "spontaneous." This boils down to controlling what is transmitted without disturbing the illusion of spontaneity. The effect can be achieved by filming an event so that it can be edited and then presenting it as if it were live. It can also take the form of staging as an extemporaneous performance what has been in fact most carefully rehearsed. Through such practices, what is supposed to be a record of actuality becomes a show. Such unspontaneous spontaneity is illustrated by the televising of rehearsed cabinet meetings during the Eisenhower administration. The professional showmanship that determined the format might not have been apparent to every viewer, but it was known and criticized by broadcasters and politicians alike. The actuality value of television was being exploited, but because the program emanated from the highest office there was no alternative to carrying it.

On the other hand, some deception is inevitably employed by every photographer who asks for a friendly wave or for the second reading of a statement so that the cameras can take it. In this instance, the subject

13. Seldes, *The Public Arts, passim.*

acts not so much as he has previously rehearsed but as coached by the newsman anxious to record the story. When Elvis Presley, the rock-and-roll singer, embarked for service in Germany with many other young men, the few fans who had gathered at the port of embarkation were not admitted to the military reservation. Yet, TV viewers expecting his farewell to become the occasion for teen-age hysteria were not to be disappointed. Others present to see off their own beaus and brothers were invited to stage a farewell—shouting "Elvis, Baby, you can't leave me," and so forth. Perhaps this was exactly the kind of send-off Presley would have received from his real fans, but it did not represent actuality.

At other times, newsmen manage through their coaching or coaxing to elicit a reaction that later builds into a major news story. Douglass Cater, in his book on the fourth estate, criticized the common practice of newsmen in approaching an official, soliciting an opinion, then quoting his words to an opponent in order to solicit a refutation.[14] The controversies that are then reported are essentially creations of the newsmen. The fact that they appear as news stories lends them actuality. A politically less controversial variant of this practice is the newsman who for the sake of a spectacle asks his subject to have a hot dog and hands him a baby to kiss. Such practices helped to "create" the per-

14. Douglass Cater, *The Fourth Branch of Government*, Boston, Houghton Mifflin, 1959.

sonality of Khrushchev that came across during his visit to the United States in 1959; much of what people saw or read of the Soviet Premier was the consequence of newsmen seeking a new angle to "tell the story."

Coached or not, those who know they are about to appear on television cannot be expected to remain indifferent to its presence. Newsmen, when asked about this, replied that "acting for the camera" was itself not reason enough to keep a scene off the air, but many of the more thoughtful saw a real dilemma. To be sure, political parties now draw up the convention agenda to achieve maximum TV exposure for certain events and personalities. But what if the cameras, simply by their presence, magnify insignificant events or permit insignificant people to stir up controversy that would otherwise scarcely exist? A commentator related an incident from the 1952 Republican convention and explained how his organization resolved it and why:

> One of our reporters was in the California caucus during a meeting. California's little MacArthur, Brigadier Herbert C. Holdridge, was also there and stirred up quite a row [though he has since sunk into oblivion]. . . . If we hadn't had the camera turned on, we might have been charged with suppression. But showing it, as we did, tended to give it greater importance than was justified. . . . That was the medium affecting the coverage; that is, Holdridge wouldn't have put on the show if it hadn't been for TV.

This particular issue was most relevant in 1967. The

mass media publicity given extremist agitators became a subject of congressional debate. The argument was that publicity-hungry militants, "leaders seeking constituencies," were so important only because the mass media had served their purposes and publicized them. Still, had the media failed to "cover" their activities, they could have made an issue of "news suppression" and the press might still have had to cover them. Creating a story that the press must cover is a time-honored tactic. But to exclude the press is to assure publicity, as when the Eisenhower forces were able to stir up an issue over the attempted exclusion of the television cameras from the National Committee hearings and thereby to create a ground swell of pressure for Eisenhower's nomination.

Conclusions

Each news organization is oriented to a standard of accurate and objective reporting of hard news. This was certainly evident in television coverage during the 1952 conventions, and it has been evident ever since. Nevertheless, the way these standards are implemented sometimes falls short of this ideal. Some practices have unanticipated consequences that, newsmen say, lie outside their responsibility. This situation may not be unique to television, but it gains added significance from the authenticity almost everyone is prone to impute to live video.

The press has always been governed in its behavior by somewhat conflicting standards. Despite the autonomy the TV news staff enjoys in covering events, it nevertheless functions as part of an organization whose primary source of revenue comes from the sale of commercial time on entertainment, rather than public affairs, programs. Yet broadcasters are also required by law to perform in the public interest, and this is the standard they invoke whenever they feel threatened by restrictive legislation. Conflict arises, as the British *Report of the Royal Commission on the Freedom of the Press* pointed out in connection with the newspaper,[15] from the disparities among the standards. The standard set for the press as the chief instrument for instructing the public on the main issues of the day, though generally similar to the one that spokesmen for the working press accept for themselves, is somewhat higher. This second standard, in turn, is still considerably higher than the standard that guides the television industry in its everyday operations as a supplier of a commodity that must always be interesting to the audience and whose chief value lies in its "novelty."

Critics frequently complain that television news in its day-to-day operations reports major events superficially, sandwiched in between entertainment and sometimes served up as entertainment. Such criticism ob-

15. Session 26, Vol. 20, 1951.

viously sees the standard of video as an instrument of education and enlightenment. It fails to take sufficient account of the competitive structure of the industry and of the limitations and constraints under which newsmen inevitably operate. In rebuttal, spokesmen for the television industry have been able to point to major achievements in live coverage as well in documentaries. Yet, even where television fails to report the news in sufficient depth, its spokesmen claim that this is the responsibility of newspapers, whose accomplishments in living up to the highest standards are certainly as uneven as those of television journalism.

That full access be granted for the televising of public events is, in principle, consistent with all three standards. It is a prerequisite for the full exploitation of the potentialities of television as a medium of education and information. It would also grant TV newsmen the same status as other members of the working press. Finally, program managers would be free to cash in on an event that seems to offer a suitable opportunity for self-dramatization as long as the costs involved can be sustained. More important than the principle, however, is the way in which it is implemented. Here our particular concern has been with the way the working press has resolved certain operating dilemmas that stem from the requirements of the story, from the press's particular conception of objectivity, and from the pressure exerted by those eager to exploit the potential power of TV for their own purposes.

The requirement hardest to live up to is that TV

should merely transmit and not influence an event. This, we believe, is impossible. Consequently, the implementation of journalistic norms must proceed from a greater awareness of the possible consequences of any kind of coverage. What is communicated is nearly always the result of "negotiation" among conflicting interests, the product of a filtering and refractive process.

V

THE INTIMATE VIEW OF POLITICS

The public, the producers of political telecasts, and political managers all seem to believe in the inherently "intimate" quality of television, a belief that is evidenced both by what they say and by what they do. The ordinary viewer and the professional TV critic appear to agree on one point: television exposes the charlatan and celebrates the real article. Typical of this viewpoint is Harriet Van Horne's assessment of a 1967 political documentary, in which the "camera's X-ray eye . . . turned, remorselessly, sometimes craftily, on each of the Republican hopefuls." One of them, Governor Ronald Reagan of California, told the television audience: "There are some things you can learn in show business that work pretty good. And one thing we've always known is that when you look at that camera in close-up, you'd better be telling the truth or that camera will reveal it." [1]

By and large, the producers of political shows have favored a format designed to bring public figure and private citizen together in an informal and cozily intimate setting, like the one which Edward R. Murrow pioneered in visiting the homes of the famous. Most candidates for high office have at least experimented with some kind of fireside chat, and now that widespread ticket-splitting has confounded some of the political analysts, it becomes all the more important for a professional politician to make friends with television.

With the advent of television, the "television personality" has come into its own. This term is used, often loosely, to designate the way a public figure "projects" himself over the air waves. Often a distinction is implied between the way the public figure comes across on TV and what he is "really" like. Thus, besides what he is himself, he has his television personality, his TV alter ego. The problem for him is how to present the proper front, the one that will best reveal his "true" measure.

1. Harriet Van Horne, "See How They Run," *New York Post,* August 19, 1967.

What produces an effective "television personality"? Who "comes across" and under what conditions? The preferred candidate, it has been said, must look competent, exude sincerity, have visual appeal, and possess any number of other vaguely defined and undefined attributes.[2] In several studies, televiewers have been asked to compare two candidates on such traits as appearance, intelligence, sincerity, humor, humility, speaking ability, friendliness, and aggressiveness. The candidates' relative standing at the beginning of the campaign and the gains and losses thereafter recorded are assumed to provide some "objective" measure of the impact of television on the personal dimension.[3] Nevertheless, these studies have contributed little to our understanding of the reasons behind the viewers' assessments or changes in the TV image.

Despite all the talk of Madison Avenue and Hollywood making over candidates, even "manufacturing" their personalities, the idea seems to persist among the public that there is a television personality that comes across to viewers by dint of sheer personal magnetism. Thus, it was generally agreed that Presidents Eisenhower and Kennedy had personalities that projected well, but that Johnson was encountering some difficulty in projecting the right kind of image. Nor are judg-

2. See Jack Gould, "The X of the Campaign—TV 'Personality,'" *New York Times Magazine*, June 22, 1952.

3. See, for example, Miami University, Department of Marketing, *The Influence of Television on the Election of 1952*.

ments of this sort confined to the United States, where politics have traditionally been more personalized. In May, 1955, when the British held their first televised election, newspapers—and the public—took a new look at figures whose names were already household words. Viewers generally rated Harold Macmillan, the new Foreign Minister (later to become Prime Minister), "urbane and telegenic," even though as many as 17 per cent among his own supporters called him "pompous." [4] Perhaps more significant, Clement Attlee, the former Prime Minister whose Labour party lost the election, was judged a television failure. He was said to come across as colorless and irritating.[5]

The popular conception of the television personality was, at the least, somewhat discredited in intensive interviews we conducted in 1952 with a sample of televiewers after both the Republican and Democratic conventions. Doubts about the inherent television appeal of particular personalities were, of course, suggested by experimental observations of spontaneous reactions to personal photographs, which psychologists have conducted in a variety of political and non-political contexts. All these experiments indicate that perceptions of faces involve elements of projection that reside in the viewer rather than in the person viewed. For instance, an experiment using pictures of obscure and unidenti-

4. *Daily Telegraph* poll.
5. *Daily Express* poll.

fied members of the British House of Commons showed that favorable traits were ascribed to those photographed when they were identified as members of one's own party.[6]

The television personality and its impact on political decisions and political life is important to all who are concerned with television as a medium of information or persuasion. But it seemed to us, on the basis of what we found in our study about viewers' reactions to the 1952 conventions, that we had to begin by reformulating the phenomenon. The "television personality" could be dissected into certain analytic elements: *television performance, political role,* and *personal image.* Beginning with an analysis of these elements, we could then look into the conditions—either inherent in the specific communications situation or in the general political life—under which political personalities may or may not project in an "intimate" light. The question to be asked was not just "Who comes across," but "Who comes across in what way, under what circumstances, and what difference does it make?"

There are a number of ways in which the television appearance of a public figure may be experienced by viewers: it can be seen as a *television performance;* as a political appearance in a *political role;* as an introduction to a human being, stirring in the viewer a *personal*

6. G. Jahoda, "Political Attitudes and Judgments of Other People," *Journal of Abnormal and Social Psychology,* XLIX (1954), 330–34.

image of the actor. Psychologists and political prognosticators have been most intrigued by the *personal image*. Yet each of these three aspects has a definite bearing on the viewer's impressions of political personalities.

Performance

A political figure on television may be judged solely in terms of his performance: whether or not the way he performs is appropriate for television and whether his performance is effective. This aspect is best exemplified, perhaps, by the approach of the professional television critic who asks whether the candidate or the government official has successfully mastered the demands of the medium. Such a judgment may be entirely independent of any political import. In fact, it may be the grudging admission of a "job well done" by a political adversary. Almost everyone agreed that the late John F. Kennedy was a sterling television performer. Several years after his death, playbacks of his "performances" at live press conferences were still considered first-rate television. In the New York mayoralty campaign of 1965, William Buckley, Conservative candidate, had no chance of winning but was sought after and applauded as a television performer guaranteed to amuse. In the same vein, many political opponents of President Eisenhower remarked on his steady improvement, under the grooming of his television advisers, as a performer.

Among the prominent figures within camera range during the conventions, some came to life only because of their performance on television. They had no prior public personalities but were picked up and "starred" by television during the convention. On the other hand, a previously well-known political figure could also make an impression as a performer, while viewers, however temporarily, dissociated the performance from the actor's personal or political role. For example, Senator Everett Dirksen made two major speeches during the course of the Republican convention; both were highly partisan and part of the maneuvering to secure the nomination for Senator Taft. Yet, despite Dirksen's obviously partisan role, viewers referred to him (immediately after the convention) chiefly as an orator, not as a Taft supporter. Whether these viewers were for Eisenhower, for Taft, or for neither, Dirksen's first speech, in which he directed a personal challenge at Governor Dewey (a chief Eisenhower supporter), was remembered as one of the memorable incidents of the convention. But the striking unanimity of praise for his forensic talents, expressed in free responses to an open-ended question, was independent of political judgments; the performance was appreciated for what it was, a well-delivered speech, irrespective of whether viewers thought it succeeded in swaying a single vote. In the words of one Eisenhower supporter, "It was the wording and actions rather than what he had to say that made the first speech a high point. Dirksen is a showman . . . but he keeps one interested." A Taftite, borrowing a phrase, called Dirksen a "silver-tongued orator."

Under what circumstances did such dissociation occur? The situation in which Dirksen starred as a performer rather than a political partisan was appropriate for the exhibition of his talents. He was a dramatic speaker, and the commentators introduced him as such. "The Taft forces are about to wheel up the big howitzer," "the real big gun orator," and so forth. Moreover, the camera, by shifting constantly between speaker and audience, helped dramatize Dirksen's appeal. His flair for histrionics was, according to what monitors and interviewees alike had to say, effective television. The speech had drama; it held the viewer's attention, whether or not he accepted its political implications.

Perhaps this documentation only highlights the obvious: some political figures perform better than others, and people may applaud or criticize the performance independently of whether or not they like the person or his politics. But the question is whether a successful TV performance in a "non-political" capacity is translatable into influence or votes. No categorical answer can be given to this crucial question. Evidently the Dirksen speech was dramatic, delivered under dramatic circumstances, and dramatized by the TV presentation. Our monitoring records and the accounts given by viewers in post-convention interviews indicate that they momentarily forgot that this was a political speech with political consequences and savored it as a first-rate performance. This dissociation raises an interesting possibility: if, under crucial circumstances, the partisan purposes of a television performance could be hidden, and especially if a good performer could operate under conditions of monopoly or near monopoly, his personality might very well achieve universal appeal. The possibilities of a TV spectacle, ostensibly above party lines and built so as to project a public figure into the forefront, appear tremendous—so long as political judgments can be held in abeyance.

This possibility conjures up notions of what a Hitler or a Castro can do in a society where the mass media are subject to strict political controls. But quite apart from this rather extreme situation, it points to the potential effectiveness with which a political figure who is at the same time a top performer can, once in power, make use of his "nonpartisan" position (as President, governor, mayor, and so forth) to mobilize support. Already, political figures seek "nonpartisan" appearances on television, as on the Jack Paar or the Johnny Carson shows, where they share the limelight and compete for attention as performers. How popularity achieved in the performer role can be translated into electoral success has recently been demonstrated by the sudden rise to national position of persons first known as personalities through their appearance in the movies, on television, and on the stage.

Political Role

A political figure may also impress because of the way in which he televises his *political role*. The competence he exhibits as he "Meets the Press," reports to the nation, or exhorts the party faithful may or may not be good television, but his appearance can be judged along political lines. The viewer may think the man shows a good grasp of his subject matter and is a capable man for a particular job. Thus, he will see him as coping with problems and wielding political influence. For example, Governor Dewey's many close-up appearances on television during the 1952 Republican convention did not, for the most part, serve to impress upon viewers his telegenic qualities either as a performer or as a "human being." Viewers "saw" only his political role. Of thirty-eight persons representing a wide range of educational and occupational backgrounds who were asked in an interview immediately after the Republican convention, "Which delegates had the most influence?," only two failed to mention Dewey. Correctly or incorrectly, almost all viewers looked upon him as the mastermind behind the Eisenhower nomination. Whether Dewey appeared as a hero or villain depended, of course, on the political preferences of the viewer; yet, as neither character did he come to life as a personality apart from that political role. Our Republicans-for-Taft remembered the convention primarily as the time when they couldn't "sink Dewey," while for Eisenhower supporters he personified the ground swell for modern Republicanism.

Eisenhower backers were visible to the television viewers in a way that Taft backers were not. Taft managers, in control of the convention machinery, were able to meet behind the main platform where they could conduct their business outside the range of the TV cameras, while much of the Eisenhower floor activity was in the open. Thus, cameras often lingered on Dewey as he operated on the floor, and commentators who talked about what cameras were showing mentioned Eisenhower managers more often than Taft managers.

The most frequent reasons given by viewers for thinking Dewey so important was that the cameras were on him a lot. As one interviewee put it, "Every time I looked it seemed I saw Dewey on the screen." He headed a big delegation, and the results showed how important he was. Some people also thought they could gauge his importance by his actions. All these explanations involved assumptions. Viewers reasoned that the cameras were on Dewey *because* he was a powerful figure. They *showed* him in control of the New York delegation, and the convention results *documented* his influence. Dewey's continued presence and the outcome testified that it was he, rather than someone else, who had engineered the nomination for Eisenhower.

The viewers themselves crowned Dewey in his role

as kingmaker. Though the commentators did point out Dewey as he appeared on the screen, an analysis of audio content indicated few direct references by commentators to Dewey as *the* power behind the throne. Moreover, throughout the convention, commentators mentioned many other delegates as power figures. In fact, the person most often mentioned as a leader of the Eisenhower forces was Senator Lodge of Massachusetts.[7] Other prominent Eisenhower backers, like Governor Langlie of Washington, Governor Thornton of Colorado, or State Senator Eastvold of Washington, made speeches and actively participated in debates. Dewey, by contrast, made no speeches and gave no official interviews. He simply appeared on the floor of the convention and on the screen.

Our intention here is not to deny that Dewey was, perhaps, the single most important Eisenhower backer at the convention. The question is simply why Dewey projected as a political figure rather than as a "person." Though his *political role* was discussed extensively by thirty-two of our viewers, the governor as a person remained a nebulous personality.[8] When viewers compared their previous opinions of Dewey to their post-convention opinions, such comparisons were made on

7. Based on references recorded by audio monitors during the entire five days of telecasting on all three networks.

8. The reactions of television critics do not necessarily coincide with those of viewers. Philip Hamburger vividly records his reactions to Dewey in "Please Clear the Aisles," *New Yorker,* July 19, 1952.

a strictly partisan basis: those for Eisenhower "thought more of him"; Taft backers "thought less of him."

What we mean to get across can be illustrated from records of monitors' "live responses" to Dewey just as he was playing his part in the proceedings.[9] Their comments did refer to the man and his feelings as well as to his role and his influence. Yet—and this seems to be the key to the depersonalization—monitors, while seeing a "cocky" or "confident," a "happy" or a "calm" Dewey, always looked for a political explanation. To them, Dewey was a man with his mind set on political goals, and his feelings warmed or chilled as these goals were approached or temporarily receded. He was never seen to smile just because he was an affable sort of fellow (or, even, because it was "good TV"), and he never shifted in his seat simply because he was tired of sitting. If he did smile, it was, in the words of a television commentator, the "smile of the cat who swallowed the canary," and all the camera close-ups could not destroy the political overtones of Dewey's every move.

That Dewey failed to emerge from the telecasts as a life-sized individual is important in view of the assumption that television, as G. D. Wiebe has suggested, casts "distant" events into an "intimate frame of

9. Pairs of monitors recorded their minute-by-minute impressions of the convention happenings on each of the three networks.

reference." [10] This alleged consequence is usually attributed to the effects of camera close-ups. There were many close-ups of Dewey, but apparently the camera could not overcome the effects of real or imagined social distance between viewer and political figure. Whether or not a man "projects" as an individual or only in his political role would seem to depend on many things, including prior stereotypy and the ambiguity of the personal emotions caught by a camera close-up.

Personal Image

Some television appearances convey to the viewer a wealth of imaginations about the human qualities of the actor. Viewers impute to the person they watch human feelings and emotions which they sympathetically share; a *personal image* is evoked. And this sympathetic closeness may be quite uninfluenced by judgments people make of his performance or his political role. This is the most popular way of thinking about the television personality. In assessing the problem President Johnson was apparently having in bridging the "credibility gap" during his second term of office, for example, political pundits often spoke of it in terms of a personal image.

Of all persons (other than potential candidates) who

10. G. D. Wiebe, "A New Dimension in Journalism," *Journalism Quarterly,* XXXI (Fall, 1954), 411–20.

played any substantial role at the Democratic convention in 1952, it was the Permanent Chairman, Sam Rayburn, long-time Speaker of the House of Representatives, whom viewers could most easily be led to talk about. After both conventions, practically the same questions were asked about the four men who at one time or other had presided over the convention—Walter Hallanan and Representative Joseph Martin for the Republicans, and Governor Dever and Sam Rayburn for the Democrats. The questions were, "What did you find out about him that you didn't know before? What sort of man do you think he is?" The responses showed that only Rayburn emerged from the convention as more than an ornament. He was frequently mentioned by viewers as one of the well-known party figures whom they "had never seen but had come to know better." They had formed an image of Rayburn the man as well as of Rayburn the chairman.

Our analysis showed that views about Rayburn's fairness and about his partisanship derived more from his role as chairman and his performance in that capacity than from any notions about his enduring personal qualities. But in dealing with what viewers thought about his ability as a chairman, one moves closer to the viewers' personal image of him. They could empathize with him as they could not with Dewey; if anyone had maintained his poise in the face of repeated challenges, it was Rayburn. Typical was this comment:

> He was cool and collected. He took quite a bit of abuse. You could see he almost had tears in his eyes when he said [after his fairness had been challenged], "Don't talk like that."

He was seen as human, patient, and composed:

> I had often wondered what kind of a man he was. In the convention he appeared to be a very patient person. My impression of him gained a little—his patience. Where others would have gotten irritated, he didn't. The way he was able to handle things!

How can we explain Rayburn's emergence into a fully rounded person, while, by comparison, other chairmen remained flat stereotypes or simply political figureheads? The difference in imagery appeared to lie more in certain elements in the telecast than in any differences among their personalities. In the first place, the viewers saw Rayburn over a longer period of time and in more trying situations. They could see what Rayburn was up against when his rulings were protested and delegates clamored for recognition all at the same time. The most dramatic moment occurred when Southern delegations were expected to walk out but—unexpectedly—South Dakota actually left in protest over Rayburn's ruling. The expected occurred in a very unexpected way and thus heightened the drama of Rayburn's personal defense before the television "jury"; he replied to South Dakota's open charge by asserting that his fairness, ability, and experience had never heretofore been questioned. It was Rayburn, and not the commentator, who told the viewer about the "justness" of his rulings. The camera close-ups of Rayburn's expression as he defended his good name gave every viewer a chance to match words with appearance, to judge how he said it. Viewers saw both the provocation and the response. The opportunity they had to "look into Rayburn's eyes" as he answered became the basis for their judgment.

In the second place, the commentary, with only passing references to his fairness, ability, and experience, did draw attention to Rayburn's personal qualities while telling the viewer nothing about the partisan role he might be playing. The commentary did not tag Rayburn with any political label (i.e., pro-Stevenson, anti-Kefauver, and so forth), and the more confused the situation and the more frequent the challenges, the more the viewer, in the absence of other guidance (as documented in Chapter III), fastened his attention on Sam Rayburn and what he would do. The relative richness of imaginations regarding him suggests that if the convention appeared at times confused—which it did—there was always Sam Rayburn at the rostrum to lend a thread of continuity to the plot. But unlike the case of Dewey, this thread involved the man and not his political role.

Certain elements in the telecast thus appear to have helped viewers develop a personal image of Rayburn the man. Yet, the tendency toward "personalization," the imputation of personal qualities to political figures, is not solely a function of the telecast; the disposition seems to be especially strong among certain types of viewers. Those who, in 1952, indicated in their pre-convention interviews that they looked forward especially to the "excitement" and conflicts of the convention were most likely to fix their attention on individual actors in terms of their "human-interest" value. They watched the conventions much as they might watch a sports event or a "soap opera." For these persons, the issue of whether Fine or Rayburn might lose his temper overshadowed any political role these people may have played. Much of what was going on, insofar as it related to political development in the convention, escaped the attention and therefore the understanding of viewers with this type of orientation.[11]

Social Distance and the Personal Image

A good television personality is certainly a useful political asset, but only rarely in a successful television campaigner will performance, role, and personal image combine to impress themselves upon the audience. The emergence of a political figure as a good performer

11. Kurt Lang and Gladys Engel Lang, "Political Participation and the Television Audience," *Social Problems*, IV (October, 1957), 107–16.

does not guarantee projection in other ways, while the candidate's personal image among the public generally depends on his political role. His supporters will have a better image of him than that held by his political adversaries. The important point is that the key to the study of successful and unsuccessful video campaigners lies in the ways in which these three elements fuse with or are dissociated from one another.

The complexities of political life, the incapacity of citizens to pass technically competent judgments on most matters that are the subject of political conflict, their inability to evaluate contradictory claims, and the projective distrust that may result place an undue premium on certain familiar traits that can be experienced and evaluated directly. "Sincerity" and "personal warmth" are among the individual qualities that are supposed to be easy to spot over TV. Television, speaking metaphorically, can indeed invite strangers into living rooms all over the country; yet, this technological miracle alone is not enough to project a figure in an "intimate" light, especially if the figure in question is a political personality. The television screen is small, and usually the persons viewing together are also few in number. But the fact that the close-up picture on the screen and the setting in which it is watched may be conducive to intimacy does not mean that intimacy is inherent in the medium.

One must differentiate between close-up and intimacy by clarifying the meaning of the latter. The social gulf separating two people can be bridged only when they are able to "meet" with a personal idea of and a feeling toward one another, to sense how the other feels toward oneself. In this proper sense, television can create no intimacy, no two-way response and exchange of feelings in which rapport is confirmed. Notwithstanding this rather obvious point, the "social distance" between viewer and viewed, though objectively great, can still be *perceived* as scarcely nonexistent. Television *may* convey events in an intimate setting; it is potentially "intimate." But to understand what makes for inferred intimacy between viewer and viewed, we have to concern ourselves not with the technical elements but the social elements involved in the perception of politics.[12]

The distinction between political role and performance, on the one hand, and personal image, on the other, can also be formulated in terms of perceived social distance between viewer and public figure. This distance involves two definitions. There is, first, the feeling of closeness and partial identification on the part of the viewer. Second, and equally important, is how close the viewer imagines that the "politician in the living room" feels to the viewer. In other words, the reduction of social distance and the projection of a personal image includes also a perception of that *other's*

12. For a contrary view, see Wiebe, "A New Dimension in Journalism."

perception—in short, it includes the viewer's idea of what a public figure is really like, how he thinks and feels toward the viewer.

Successful projection seems, in the short run, a consequence of two main elements: the situation in which the public figure is shown, and the preconceptions and imagery about him already disseminated among viewers. In the following paragraphs, we present some hypotheses as to when a political figure becomes familiar, in the sense of a lessening of social distance, and as to when he "projects" only as a "politician" or as a performer.

(1) Where a public figure delivers a spectacular performance, that performance may have a great immediate impact; yet, barring other conditions which would project him in another light, he will be appreciated simply as a performer, a successful orator, an effective keynoter, a smooth operator, and so forth. The reason would seem to involve the prevalent distrust with which politics and politicians are viewed, and according to which performances are defined as primarily manipulative in intent. In this way, a dissociation between the momentary involvement and its political overtones becomes established and is maintained as a barrier in the way of direct persuasion via the mass media.

(2) If a political figure is shown in a relatively unfamiliar situation and no clear explanation of his role is offered, he is apt to be recognized (unless already known) as the mere embodiment of some appro-

priate stereotypy: just another general, a typical big-city boss, or the like.

(3) An important figure—as in the case of Dewey and most other presidential candidates—will, if already known for his political functions, tend to be perceived on television in that political role irrespective of the number of close-ups or the home viewing situation.

(4) To the degree that a public figure is shown in a series of actions that allow a viewer to note his personal responses, the person televised is more likely to project as a "human-interest" figure and perhaps as a "person," but only if two conditions are met: (a) There must be no strong political preconceptions on the part of the viewer which interfere; thus, one of our interviewees interpreted the absence from the 1952 convention of Stevenson's oldest son (then getting his Marine boot training) as evidence that he "hated his father," that is, she "saw" the absent son, not the two who were present. (b) The camera and commentary must highlight personal reactions and personality rather than possible political overtones.

Besides the influence of such predispositions, however widely dispersed, there are certain more general social conditions which may promote the emergence of public figures "intimately known" by the masses. These involve: the nature of prevalent political controversy; the existence of distrust; and prior mass media build-up.

(5) The impact of a personal image is greatest when public discussion is relatively lacking in "class" or

"interest" type issues. When there appears to be fundamental consensus in society, public controversy is likely to center on personalities, on who is the "best man" to lead them toward the common ends, thus making "use of symbols which assemble emotions after they have been detached from their ideas." [13]

(6) In a context in which political ethics are assumed to be rather low, the purely personal qualities ("character") of political figures tend to be stressed. This "context of distrust," as Robert K. Merton [14] has called it, requires the audience to political television—and citizens in general—to find some anchoring point in which to believe, and it may well be found in the personal image of a public figure that becomes concretized through the use of television.

(7) A television personality with full-blown political appeal is rarely the result of television appearances themselves; its emergence and longevity generally depend on media interpretation. Even where hitherto unknown and unmarked public figures attain prominence through television, they are not left to themselves once they become known. Television "performance" alone, it would appear, is not directly translatable into votes, for political allies and opponents, newspapers and public relations agencies, and everyone else will pro-

13. Walter Lippman, *The Phantom Public,* New York, Harcourt, Brace, 1925, p. 47.

14. Robert K. Merton, *Mass Persuasion,* New York, Harper, 1946, p. 142.

ceed to applaud or decry the man (and his appearances) until some image is formed that undoubtedly comes to overshadow the initial impact and give it a new significance, even among those few who may have been exposed to the "original." Each subsequent appearance then validates the image.

The importance of a build-up may be documented from even a cursory examination of news coverage of the television campaign in 1952. One notes a constant concern with the efficacy of General Eisenhower's appearances. After each telecast, reporters asked and answered whether or not the *real* Eisenhower had come across. What was said during the press conference, speech, or interview was less remarked upon than how well the general had performed. Behind the picture itself there seemed to lurk a picture of the "real Eisenhower" and whether or not the telecast did justice to it. The image of Eisenhower which had been built up by the press prior to television and which existed outside of television undoubtedly did much to make his video roles effective, and, despite performances that were dubbed "flops," the successes must have served to reassure his public that there was an Eisenhower who was sometimes left behind in the stage props and production.

In the case of Adlai Stevenson, the issue never arose. The press rarely judged the adequacy of his performance in these terms. A certain "aloofness," a certain distance maintained between Stevenson and his audience, a failure to "project" in a particularly personal way were often said to mark his appearances. Yet the failure of Stevenson to project himself in an intimate light (if this was so) rarely gave impetus to a search for the "real" Stevenson. It is true, of course, that in 1956 newspapers readers often heard that Stevenson the campaigner was not "true" to himself; it was a "changed" Stevenson who talked to television viewers. But the "real" Stevenson for whom critics looked was not the "real" man behind the public image but the television performer and political figure whom the media, all together, helped to fashion in 1952.

Finally, we can neither conclude nor imply from our findings that television makes no difference in the picture the public may gain of political personalities. Most important, there is a widespread belief in the intimacy of television, and this, in itself, makes a difference. When the formats of political telecasts are adapted to this belief, they emphasize the personal qualities of the politician rather than his purely political qualifications, or how well equipped he is to handle a particular role. At the same time, viewers believe they have "seen for themselves," and their visual impressions suggest to them the "real" personal qualities of the familiar face. In all of this, the contribution of television is made through its sensory realism, through the emphasis it places on symbols directly accessible to experience. The heterogeneity of views on complex policy matters and public problems can be factored down to simple alternatives. The search for "truth" becomes a search for "trust." Principles and methods become less important than "sincerity." Such a criterion is all-encompassing. This seems but a final step in the historical process of mobilizing mass opinion, culminating in what Lippmann some thirty years ago already referred to as "the intensification of feeling and a degradation of significance." [15] The particular television performance may have little to do with the "television personality" of any one individual, but television has succeeded in making the "television personality" itself a significant factor in political life.

15. Lippmann, *The Phantom Public,* p. 48.

VI

ORDEAL BEFORE TELEVISION: THE KENNEDY-NIXON DEBATES

In 1960, presidential candidates Richard M. Nixon and John F. Kennedy appeared together before the television cameras four times—altogether four hours—within a span of four weeks to answer questions put to them by a panel of four newsmen. These "debates" were major campaign events. They were broadcast live. In the first broadcast, on September 26 from Chicago, and on October 7 in Washington, D.C., and October 21 in New York, the two men spoke from the same studio. On October 13, when Nixon was in Los Angeles and Kennedy in New York, they met each other at a distance—through a split-screen technique.

Judged by the audience they reached, the broadcasts were a huge success. Between 65 and 70 million watched any one telecast; somewhere between 85 and 120 million were estimated to have witnessed at least one of the four.

Reminiscent of the famous Lincoln-Douglas debates a century before, these four programs were everywhere referred to as the Great Debates. Still, to label them "debates" is not entirely accurate. The programs conformed only superficially to the format of a debate. For one thing, the two candidates neither challenged nor addressed one another directly. Instead, reporters took turns asking questions which, according to the rules, had to be directed alternately at each of the two candidates. There were strict time limitations. Two and a half minutes were allowed for a direct reply, at the end of which the other "debater" had one and a half minutes for rebuttal. The enforcement of these rules was left to a newsman who served as moderator and also introduced and closed the program.

The first and last programs were restricted to specific topics: domestic policy and foreign affairs, respectively. In these two "debates," but not in the others, each candidate received eight minutes for an opening statement defining his position. Reporters then pursued these same topics with their questions, whereas in the other "debates" they were free to range over any topics they wished.

The television appearances of Kennedy and Nixon were certainly a major innovation, but the idea was not nearly as new. In 1956, President Eisenhower, running for re-election, had refused a challenge from his opponent, Governor Stevenson, to debate on television before a national audience. Soon after, support for such a face-to-face confrontation during the next campaign began to build up. A main stumbling block, however, was a clause in the Federal Communications Act of 1934. Section 315 of that act required any broadcaster who offered free time to a political candidate to offer "free and equal time" to every other candidate for the same office. The Federal Communications Commission had interpreted this clause literally. The requirement could not be met simply by an offer of equal time to the *major* candidates; the offer had to include, in fact, every candidate. But consider what this meant: in 1960, there were sixteen officially declared candidates seeking the presidency. They included such perennial contenders as the nominees of the Socialist Labor party, the Prohibition party, and the American Vegetarian party, as well as some new hopefuls like the nominees of the American Beat Consensus, the Tax Cut party, and the Afro-American Unity party. Obviously, only a very small circle of the electorate could even have identified these candidates, yet all could have pressed for "free and equal" time.

Despite their eagerness to carry the televised debates, the networks clearly did not wish to assume the costs of granting similar time to the whole gamut of legally qualified candidates. Hence, during the winter and spring of 1960, they sought, unsuccessfully, the abolition of Section 315. They did succeed, however, in extracting from Congress, just before it recessed in August, a temporary suspension of the "equal time" rule.

Once the legal obstacle was removed, further progress depended on the ability of the interested parties to agree on the time, number, and format of the debates. Viewpoints on the purposes of the debates diverged considerably, and the final resolution was a compromise. The major interest of the networks was in a show that would effectively dramatize the capabilities of television. Nixon's managers wanted a single debate with cross-questioning between the two candidates in classic debate tradition. Kennedy's representatives asked for five debates, hoping to give their lesser-known candidate the maximum possible exposure.

At the beginning of the campaign, Kennedy had clearly been the underdog. In contrast to Nixon, who had won the Republican nomination with almost no serious challenge, Kennedy had been forced to wage a pre-convention campaign against Senator Hubert Humphrey of Minnesota and then stave off a last-minute, emotion-packed try by Stevenson backers to secure a third nomination for their man. Kennedy, therefore, had considerable fence-mending to do. Many

Democrats felt that he had "bought" rather than earned the nomination. They were not yet ready to give him their full support. Nixon had been spared all this. Besides, he could, as a member of the outgoing administration, cash in on the experience gained during a number of missions abroad. His prestige, assumedly, went beyond party lines. And it must be noted that though Nixon was just about four years older than Kennedy, neither "youth" nor lack of experience was ever cited—as in the case of Kennedy—to show Nixon's unsuitability for the presidency. The issues mentioned here were not, of course, the only ones, but they were the ones most relevant in assessing the impact of the televised debates.

Immediately after Kennedy's narrow election victory, observers began to suggest that television had been the undoing of Richard M. Nixon. On the Monday following the election, Kennedy himself was reported to have said, "It was TV more than anything else that turned the tide." [1]

1. Theodore H. White, *The Making of the President 1960,* New York, Pocket Books paperback ed., 1962, p. 353.

A Panel Study of Viewer Reactions

Our study of the televised debates made no attempt to pass judgment on the accuracy of this diagnosis. This is because an electoral campaign consists of many events and involves many overlapping issues. To disentangle the influence of any single factor (event or issue) on the outcome of an election is always difficult. To do so with the 1960 campaign begins to border on logical absurdity. The closeness of the Kennedy victory—he won by less than twenty thousand votes—showed that to win he needed every single one of the breaks he got. His victory was attributable only to a concatenation of all the factors working in his favor. He needed the votes of Southern Negroes and got them, apparently through his intervention for Martin Luther King when King was sentenced by a Georgia court (on a technicality) to four months of hard labor. The support of New York's liberal Democrats—equally important—was obtained through the efforts of Eleanor Roosevelt, Herbert Lehman, and others in the party's reform wing there. Labor's enthusiastic help everywhere supplied a crucial balance, and the rise of unemployment that fall undoubtedly helped make Kennedy's campaign rhetoric about "moving ahead" more persuasive than it could otherwise have been. There is no way of showing that the TV debates rather than some other event (or factor), supplied the decisive margin of victory.

The issue of the impact of such televised debates must, moreover, be posed against a background of what has been fairly well established about the impact of mass communications during political campaigns and not just in the 1960 presidential election.[2] The mass political fare generally has two effects: (1) it increases the relevancy of political identifications which people use to make up their minds, and (2) it promotes consistency between voting preferences and the images of candidates, opinions on issues, and so forth, through which individual voters support these preferences. Campaign events can have a clear influence on the outcome if they somehow crystallize the votes of one side more strongly than those of the other, or if they bring about mass switches—the latter is much less likely.

The potential for change during the span of a campaign is severely limited by the fact that most voters have closed minds even before the campaign officially opens. Many persons simply direct their attention so as to bolster a preference already held. Generally speaking, there is little inclination to seek out deliberately and to weigh carefully and dispassionately the viewpoints and arguments presented by both sides. Hence, the televised debates differed from the usual campaign communications in several respects:

2. Among other summaries of the impact are Bernard R. Berelson, Paul F. Lazarsfeld, and W. N. McPhee, *Voting*, Chicago, University of Chicago Press, 1954, appendix, and Eugene Burdick and A. J. Brodbeck, ed., *American Voting Behavior*, Glencoe, Ill., Free Press, 1959, Chapters 12 and 13.

First, "double exposure" was inherent in their very format; there was no practical way for a viewer to expose himself to the personality of one candidate without the other, or to listen to the arguments presented by him without surmising at the same time how well they stood up in the rebuttal.

Second, it stands to reason that the debates, which emphasized the give-and-take between the two men, would have their main impact on the images of the candidates' personalities.

Third, novelty, advance publicity, viewing habits, and perhaps the unique suitability of television for the debate format combined to attract audiences considerably larger than those usually exposed to campaign telecasts. The debates overshadowed most other campaign events.

Ours was a small-scale panel study of ninety-five New York viewers. In this kind of study, the same persons (i.e., the members of a panel) who are interviewed the first time are later reinterviewed. We aimed at interviewing every one of our respondents at some length three different times: late in September just before the first debate, then immediately after that debate, and again after the fourth and last encounter.[3] These interviews enabled us to detail how vivid, new perceptions of the candidates arose in response to this double expo-

3. Altogether, 104 persons were interviewed before or after the debates. Ninety-seven were interviewed before the first debate, but two of them could not be reinterviewed. Seven others were interviewed only after the first debate. Statistics were based only on those ninety-five persons interviewed three times.

sure. They also indicated how these sometimes disturbing perceptions were handled by viewers and related to to—or isolated from—their vote decisions. Although changes in voting intention unquestionably constitute the clearest measure of impact (and interviews did give us information about this), the study focused on how the debates influenced the images and comparisons of the two candidates by viewers.

On purely statistical grounds, this sample warrants no inferences about the same effects in a larger population, national or local. Twenty-four of the interviews were self-interviews by college seniors enrolled in a mass communications course at a nonresident New York City campus. The other seventy-one were obtained by these same students from voters outside the college community. Selection procedures were designed to give us a fairly even distribution of potential Kennedy and Nixon supporters and as wide a range as possible on a number of other characteristics.[4]

The observations illustrate the processes underlying

4. Of ninety-seven interviewed before the first debate, thirteen were under twenty-one and too young to vote; twenty-three were between twenty-one and twenty-four and thus first voters; nineteen were between twenty-five and thirty-four; thirty-three were between thirty-five and fifty-four; and seven were fifty-five and over. The sample contained fifty persons of Jewish origin, twenty-six Protestants, eighteen Catholics, and three who gave no religion; seven persons added on the second wave were Catholic. The socioeconomic level of the sample was somewhat above average and contained, as noted, a large number of students. Persons gainfully employed divided rather evenly among three groups: professions, managerial, and white-collar employees; sales personnel and small businessmen; and blue-collar workers. Of those who voted in 1956 and responded to a question about how they voted, 44 per cent had voted Republican and 56 per cent Democratic. Asked which party they belonged to or "identified" with, 59 per cent responded "Democratic," 21 per cent "Republican," with the

communication effects as they occur in individuals. Among this panel there was an immediate and dramatic improvement in the Kennedy image after the first debate. The impression he made was considerably better than that made by Nixon. Both the absolute advantage Kennedy enjoyed and the gains he scored were particularly great among those who, before the debates, had not as yet decided how to vote and among those who identified themselves as independent voters.[5] These dramatic changes in imagery were, however, *not* accompanied by shifts in voting intentions of anywhere near comparable proportions. These are, to a degree, independent. Consequently, we will take up first the impact of the debates on voting intentions, which reflect decisions made, and second, the manner in which new perceptions entered into candidate images and were then related to electoral choices.

Changes in Voting Intentions

Among the shifts in voting intentions, one can distinguish three types: *Crystallization* represents a movement from being "undecided" or even ready not to vote at all

---

others declaring themselves Independent or unaffiliated, or refusing to answer. In traditionally Democratic New York City, most of the "Independents" revealed themselves to be, by voting record, attitudes, and so forth, inclined toward the Republicans.

5. For similar results, see Elihu Katz and Jacob J. Feldman, "The Debates in the Light of Research: A Survey of Surveys," in S. Kraus, ed., *The Great Debates*, Bloomington, University of Indiana Press, 1962, pp. 173–223.

toward a clear-cut preference for one of the two candidates. *Switching* is a movement from one candidate to the other; but a switch that is temporary or a weakening of commitment without an actual change to the other candidate constitutes *wavering.* Table 1 summarizes the aggregate change within the panel over the period in which the debates took place. No evidence was collected on how or whether respondents actually did vote in November.

Table 1 Voting Intentions*

	Before Debates		After 1st Debate		After 4th Debate	
Decided for Kennedy	37	39	47	53	52	56
Leaning toward Kennedy	2		6		4	
Undecided		23		12		7
Leaning toward Nixon	2	33	2	30	1	32
Decided for Nixon	31		28		31	
		95		95		95

* Based on respondents with whom three interviews were completed.

As shown in Table 1, the largest gain for Kennedy came from the crystallization of intent. It illustrates his success in rallying to his side a larger number of the uncommitted than Nixon. After the fourth debate, the preference of twenty-three persons initially uncommitted were thus distributed: fifteen either for Kennedy or clearly leaning his way; three for Nixon, five still undecided or determined not to vote. The decisive shift to Kennedy came right after the first debate, when eight decided for Kennedy and four more indicated a definite leaning toward him.

There were only four switchers. Three of them went from Nixon to Kennedy and one from Kennedy to Nixon. The Kennedy switchers defected (or at least began to lean) to Kennedy right after the first debate; all three said they had been impressed with the performance. The pro-Nixon switch recorded by the end of the debate series was not evident in any way after the initial television encounter.

Six persons initially for Nixon wavered. One of these moved into the undecided group after the first debate, and one after the series was over. The other four weakened in their preference but did not end up as undecided: they either continued to lean toward Nixon or returned to Nixon after the last debate. Only one Kennedy supporter wavered in that he grew less certain of his preference after the first debate but continued to lean toward Kennedy.

All told, then, there were twenty-two changes within our panel—eighteen crystallizers plus four switchers. Over 80 per cent of these changes (eighteen out of twenty-two, to be exact) benefited Kennedy. Apparently he was able to tap a traditionally Democratic potential of persons who, for a variety of reasons, had deferred their decision. His added strength came largely from weak

Democratic party identifiers, that is, persons who considered themselves independent but acknowledged a general preference for Democrats. Among eleven weak Democratic identifiers who changed to Kennedy, nine had been too young to vote in 1956 and two had defected to vote for Eisenhower in 1956. Five others who changed to Kennedy were self-styled Democrats; their switch in the course of the debate was a return to that allegiance. Only two of the votes gained by Kennedy can be said to have come from across party lines: one of these was a Republican, the other a self-styled Independent; both had voted for Eisenhower in 1956.

Nixon, on the other hand, won two votes from persons who favored Stevenson in 1956: one from a "Democrat" who had previously voted Republican, and another from a new voter who thought of himself as Independent.

When viewed against the voter's party identification and voting history, very few of the intra-campaign switches contradict the voter's political past. The majority of switchers were merely responding to inclinations that had clearly been present earlier and might have been activated even without the debates. Nixon failed to consolidate sufficiently the inroads Eisenhower had made into the large Democratic potential, the heritage of the New Deal era—inroads that any Republican had to maintain or expand if he were to win. As the campaign progressed, among this panel of voters Kennedy gained votes at a 4 to 1 ratio. The debates, being the major and perhaps the most dramatic campaign event, hastened the polarization of the electorate but not, as far as our evidence goes, along lines contrary to tradition.

The evidence from this study, as well as from others,[6] shows that the first debate accelerated the movement toward Kennedy and strengthened pro-Democratic commitments. Nevertheless, one cannot definitively conclude that these changes would not have occurred in any event, with or without the debates. Kennedy had already been making headway among voters, and it is possible that these votes would have crystallized as they did simply as a function of time. One thing is clear, however: the debates provided new arguments for supporting Kennedy and, therefore, strengthened convictions. The public, in particular, thought the debates the most important element that led to Kennedy's victory. Perhaps the same amount of enthusiastic support for his campaign would not have been forthcoming without this dramatic confrontation between the two candidates. No one will ever be able to tell.

Pre-Debate Images

Voting preference is usually linked in various degrees with party identification, orientation to political issues,

6. Katz and Feldman, "The Debates in the Light of Research."

and images of the candidates. Each of these variables exerts some independent influence on the vote, and when all three are consistent—as when traditional party identification goes with a preference for that party's candidate and there is agreement with his stand on issues—one can predict with a high degree of reliability how a person will vote.[7] Issue orientation and candidate preferences are clearly more variable and volatile than party identifications. They usually account for "cross-overs" between elections. And since it can be said with some assurance that the debates highlighted the competitive performance of the two candidates, one can also confidently say that any changes in voting preferences resulting from the debates were mediated primarily through changes in the images of the candidates.

Nixon had used his association with Eisenhower, but he had also been working hard to build up his image as a statesman in his own right. He had already demonstrated his skill as a debater by the apparent cool confidence with which he had delivered his famous Checkers speech (see Chapter I). More recently, he had received much publicity from his "kitchen debate" with Premier Khrushchev. Television newsreels and press photographs had prominently featured an episode from the Vice President's trip to Russia, showing him with his

7. See Angus Campbell, Gerald Gurin, and Warren E. Miller, *The Voter Decides,* New York, Harper, 1954, and Angus Campbell, *et al., The American Voter,* New York, Wiley, 1960.

finger pointed at the Premier, apparently scoring a point. Nixon himself reports that Mikoyan had taken him aside afterward in order to compliment him: "I reported to Mr. Khrushchev . . . that you were very skillful in debate, and you proved it again today." [8]

Kennedy had also been in the public eye. He had emerged from World War II as a a war hero and then served in Congress for some fourteen years, first in the House and then in the Senate. His book, *Profiles in Courage,* had been a best-seller, his marriage to Jacqueline Bouvier a major social event.

The image viewers had of Nixon *before the debates* was, not unexpectedly, much sharper and clearer than the one they had of Kennedy. Nixon had held *national* elective office and, as a result, was far better known. Seventy per cent of our panel said they were "more familiar" with Nixon; 18 per cent said they were equally familiar (or unfamiliar) with both; only 12 per cent thought they knew Kennedy better. Yet, certain well-defined images of each candidate were widely shared by the panel.

The image of Nixon. First, the impression that the vice presidency entailed more responsibility and afforded better preparation for the presidency than serving in the Senate was accepted, at least tacitly, even by most Democrats. Second, Nixon was remembered as a roving political ambassador who had dealt with angry mobs in

8. Richard M. Nixon, *Six Crises,* Garden City, Doubleday, 1962, p. 258.

South America and debated with Khrushchev in Russia, though viewers assessed these accomplishments differently. Third, Nixon's formidability as a TV personality and debater was acknowledged by both those for and against his candidacy. Finally, respondents saw in Nixon an experienced and skilled politician; even opponents who heartily disliked him doubted that he would ever again resort to tactics which had been successful against past political opponents, tactics which they distrusted and which made them distrust Nixon.

The image of Kennedy. The Kennedy image was simpler but also somewhat more "personal"; it was less closely tied to his past political efforts, and so Kennedy, unlike Nixon, emerged more as a "man" than as a "political man." The dominant image of the senator, even among many who intended to vote against him, was of a "fine young man" with some potential. He was most often viewed as competent and cool, an ambitious young fellow who knew how to build a political organization, as evidenced by his nomination. Both those for and against him widely referred to Kennedy as "vigorous" or "vital." Doubts were voiced, however, about his convictions; many considered him "snobbish" and were highly suspicious of the political influence of his family and of his Catholicism. As an aside, it may be mentioned that the most unfriendly image of Kennedy was shared largely by the Catholic Republicans interviewed, of whom two were among the most outspoken in their opposition to a Catholic, especially a Catholic such as Kennedy, in the White House.

Expectations Before the Debate

People looked forward to the debates as a match of the candidates' forensic skills—their ability, as it was so often expressed, to "put their views across." The partisan hoped to see his candidate perform effectively and thereby improve his chance of winning. Most of those interviewed thought the debates might affect the voting decisions of others but doubted that they would have any effect on their own thinking.

There was, however, a significant difference between the expectations of Nixon partisans and Kennedy partisans (Table 2). Two-thirds of Nixon's thirty partisans

Table 2 Expectations and Actual Performance in First Debate *

Political Preference Before 1st Debate	Nixon Better	About the Same	Kennedy Better	Don't Know, No Answer
	Expectations of Performance			
Nixon (30)	21	6	3	0
Undecided (22)	9	8	4	1
Kennedy (39)	11	12	13	3
Total	41	26	20	4
Per Cent	45	29	22	4
	Actual Performance			
Nixon (30)	8	10	12	0
Undecided (22)	0	2	20	0
Kennedy (39)	2	9	28	0
Total	10	21	60	0
Per Cent	11	23	66	....

* Six of ninety-seven respondents with whom pre-debate interviews were completed said they had not watched the first debate. The comparison remains essentially unaffected by whether or not the six non-viewers are included.

felt confident of their candidate's superior debating skills; only three thought Kennedy would do better. Even among Kennedy partisans, Nixon was considered a formidable opponent. A reading of the interviews reveals that only a few Kennedy supporters had real confidence that their man would be a match for Nixon. In the way they evaded a flat prediction, many implied that they were worried by Nixon's reputation as a political infighter.

Those who thought they "might be influenced" by the debates put a special stress on the image the candidates would project. A number intended to look specifically for "the way a candidate answered," apart from what he might say. "I want to see," said one, "whether they hem and haw before they answer, whether they mean what they say, and whether they are sincere." Others said they would look for signs of knowledgeability and an ability to stand up "courageously."

Finally, many who were undecided and a number of party faithfuls lukewarm to the candidate said they would seek information on how the candidates stood on important issues. They expected that the debate format, because it offered a unique opportunity for the "instantaneous reply," would force the candidates into clear-cut statements of policy and expose past records.

The First Debate

The first historic encounter took place in a Chicago TV studio on September 26, 1960, at 9:30 P.M. (EST). Veteran newsman Howard K. Smith, in his capacity as moderator, introduced the program and the four reporters on the panel. Kennedy had drawn the first position and, consequently, led off with his opening statement. Paraphrasing Lincoln, he asked whether the world could exist half-slave and half-free. All he said, more or less, led up to his now familiar concluding phrase: "I think it's time America started moving again."

Nixon answered his opponent by agreeing with the general goals Kennedy had set forth. To stay ahead, he said, the nation would have to continue moving ahead. The point he disputed was that America, under Eisenhower, had been standing still.

Subsequent comments on the first debate seemed to indicate that—to paraphrase Lincoln once more—the nation did not long remember what they said there, but it did remember how they looked when they said it. People wondered, in particular, why Nixon's performance had not lived up to expectations. Had the room been too hot? Was he still ailing from the infected knee for which he had undergone treatment in July?

Controversy centered on how certain production details might have affected the ability of the candidates to project themselves.[9] Extreme care had been taken with the production. A new set had been built with special

9. A careful and objective "inside" account of the production is that by Herbert A. Seltz and Richard D. Yoakam, "Production Diary of the Debates," in Kraus, *The Great Debates*, pp. 73–126.

attention to background color and lighting. There had been requests from the managers of both candidates, especially from Nixon's, about the placement of lights and what shots *not* to take. Some of these remained subject to discussion for years.

After the first debate, a newspaper story charged that a makeup man had deliberately sabotaged Nixon's appearance. It now seems firmly established that Nixon himself vetoed the recommendation that he wear any makeup beyond some powder to cover his "five-o'clock shadow." If Nixon looked hot and uncomfortable, this was at least partly due to his own production advisers. Their demands for additional lights overrode the objections of CBS's senior lighting director. They also requested that left profile shots of Nixon be avoided and that no reaction shots be taken while the candidate was wiping perspiration from his face. Yet, one reaction shot caught him sweating and apparently glaring at the camera. Kennedy looked youthful, healthy, and suntanned by comparison.

Nixon's own comment on these events of the first debate was that he had made a "basic mistake." He had concentrated "too much on substance and not enough on appearance." While he denied what some supporters contended—that he was not feeling up to par physically—he indicated that he had, in fact, been quite rundown but didn't know it at the time. The camera, like a microscope, had revealed his true physical condition to the audience even before he himself had become aware of it.[10] Before the second debate, Nixon put on five pounds.

Impact of the First Debate

The impact of the first debate was quite dramatic. Eighty-nine per cent of our panel who watched or heard the first debate thought Kennedy had bested Nixon or at least had fought him to a draw (Table 2). This seems also to have been the predominant reaction throughout the country. A national sample of approximately one thousand viewers interviewed by the Gallup organization during the period September 24 to October 4, 1960, found that about twice as many thought Kennedy did better than thought Nixon did better. The single most important result of the debate lay in its destruction of the image, so widely held, of Richard Nixon as champion debater and television politician *par excellence*. This re-evaluation of the comparative ability of the two men as performers is what helped crystallize the vote of undecideds and caused partisans to revise their images of the men as persons and as presidential timber.

Changes in the images of candidates as *persons* mainly reflected viewers' political preferences. But, as Table 3 shows, Kennedy scored net gains, creating a more favorable personal image for himself. His unexpectedly able

10. Nixon, *Six Crises*, p. 341.

performance dissolved many doubts about his maturity and experience, even among Nixon supporters. By contrast, Nixon's personal image deteriorated dramatically among Democrats and the undecided; moreover, five out of thirty Nixon supporters had a less favorable view of Nixon the person. Still, while some Kennedy supporters found Nixon less well informed than they had supposed, the Nixon supporters, who had thought their candidate very well informed before the debate, afterward found him even better informed. Thus, among the viewers as a whole (as shown in Table 3), the personal

Table 3 Change in Candidates' Image After First Debate (Percentages) *

	Better	Unchanged	Worse	No Answer
Kennedy personal image	45	45	5	4
Nixon personal image	20	47	29	4
Kennedy informedness	41	53	3	3
Nixon informedness	14	67	11	8

* Based on ninety-one respondents. Rounded to nearest whole number.

image of Nixon deteriorated, but the judgment of Nixon's informedness remained pretty much as before.

A judgment of overall attitude toward the two candidates was made from answers to questions about what viewers had discovered about each man—how able he was, what he stood for, how he had voted, how he performed, and so forth. Table 4 uses the categories "Improvement" and "Deterioration" with regard to this *overall* image. The categories "Favorable (Unfavorable)

Table 4 Changes in Overall Valuation of Candidates After Debate

Political Preference Before 1st Debate	Improvement	Favorable Image Validated	No Change	Unfavorable Image Validated	Deterioration
			Kennedy Evaluations		
Nixon (30)	10	1	7	12	0
Undecided (22)	11	0	9	2	0
Kennedy (39)	19	15	4	0	1
Total	40	16	20	14	1
Per Cent *	45	18	22	15	1
			Nixon Evaluations		
Nixon (30)	1	16	7	0	6
Undecided (22)	2	0	9	3	8
Kennedy (39)	6	0	13	14	6
Total	9	16	29	17	20
Per Cent *	10	18	32	19	22

* Rounded to nearest whole number.

Image Validated" were added to indicate persons whose overall judgment changed but only insofar as they became more certain in their judgment than they had been. The potential for improvement was limited by the fact that each candidate entered the debates with a fund of good will among his supporters; the potential for deterioration was limited by the hostility each already encountered among the opposition.

As expected, many respondents merely validated a

favorable image of their own candidate and an unfavorable image of his opponent. What interested us was, first, a general improvement in the overall impression of Kennedy, an improvement that was very marked for those initially uncommitted, only somewhat less marked among Kennedy partisans, and extended even to supporters of Nixon. Again, what was true of our viewers was true of viewers throughout the nation. Among a test audience recruited by the Gallup organization in the Trenton, New Jersey, area, the proportion who held a "very" favorable image of Kennedy increased 16 per cent following the debate compared with an increase of 4 per cent for Nixon. The Survey Research Center (University of Michigan) found that among Independents, favorable responses to Kennedy after the debates were twice as frequent as favorable responses to Nixon.[11] The second interesting result was that, because most Nixon supporters merely validated an initially favorable image while five indicated less favorable impressions, the image of Nixon held by the panel as a whole deteriorated. Third, gains made by Nixon among Kennedy supporters are noteworthy even though they were not large enough to offset the trend, that is, they occurred among a group whose image to begin with had been strongly negative.

11. Press releases by the two organizations.

Cumulative Impact

Reactions to the first encounter set the tone. The images of the candidates, once firmed up in response to that initial debate, changed very little thereafter, even though many of these impressions were clearly not in line with voting intentions. Thus, both candidates had scored some gains among persons supporting their opponents. One might have expected these viewers, whose intentions were not reinforced, but even undermined, by the first debate, to gear their subsequent communication behavior so as to bring candidate preference and image in line.[12] There are several ways to do this besides changing one's preference: by refusing to watch further debates, by turning to sources of information more favorable to one's candidate, and by continuing to look in subsequent debates for clues reaffirming one's original convictions.

Because of alternative ways of reducing dissonance (other than avoiding the debates), among our panel there was no evidence that dissonance introduced by the first debate led either to more or less viewing of the debates that followed. The number of debates watched was unrelated to (a) initial candidate preference, (b) judgment of who had won the first debate, (c) amount of change in image, or (d) education of the viewer.

12. The theoretical argument for this expectation is found in L. Festinger, *A Theory of Cognitive Dissonance,* Evanston, Ill., Row, Peterson, 1957.

But responses after the last debate showed rather clearly how much people had come to rely on interpretations they had read in newspapers and news magazines, usually publications reflecting their own views. Viewers' later observations showed considerable stereotypy and lacked the originality that had characterized responses after the first debate. From this it appears that journalistic interpretations and personal conversations supplied a frame of reference permitting the assimilation of information from subsequent debates without stirring new doubt or conflict.

Another way of reducing strain between image and voting preference involved a reassessment of the various elements that made up a candidate's political personality and of their relevance to electoral choice. The televised debates dramatized competitive performance. A viewer whose image of Nixon's prowess as a debater had suffered a serious blow could, from there on, deny that this was any reflection on Nixon's qualifications for the office. On the contrary, he might even be drawn more strongly to Nixon by sympathy and react negatively to a candidate too quick with his tongue.

To stress the importance of candidate image here is not to ignore the stability introduced by party identification and by the network of associations that activate the electorate at election time. In the rhythmic pattern of politics, party images often become blurred between national elections. The political personality chosen by each party to head the ticket and to be the spokesman of party policy plays a crucial role in the electoral campaign, which is aimed at moving party identifications back into the foreground of attention and refurbishing the party image. The party, temporarily united behind the candidate, appeals through him to the electorate. But the "strain toward consistency" among voters' images of personal self-interest, national interest, party policies, and so forth, includes the image of the party candidate.

The image of a political personality projected by television has been shown (Chapter V) to depend upon evaluations of three component elements: his television *performance,* here as a "debater"; his fitness for the *political role* in which he is cast, here that of candidate aspiring to the presidency; and his *personal image*—what kind of human being is he? what is he like as a "real" person? The appeal of a political personality is a function of the way the man on the screen projects along each of these dimensions and whether they are related or isolated in the viewer's cognition. The relationship among these elements, as well as the relationship between these elements and political decisions, is similar in certain respects to the relationship between information and attitudes on which the information supposedly bears. New or negative information does not necessarily mean a reassessment of pertinent attitudes. Neither does a changed perception of performance necessarily carry over to perception of the "man" performing, and so forth. The rest of this chapter takes up this question of how new cognitive elements introduced so vividly in the first debate were dealt with by viewers.

The essential question is why dramatic changes in evaluations were followed by less dramatic changes in voting intentions.

Performance, Personal Image, Political Role

Even though partisans wanted their man to "win" so that they could reassure themselves and convince others, few viewers, whether partisan or uncommitted, would have seriously proposed before the first debate that a candidate's ability to score points under the rules agreed on for that debate was a test of fitness for office. Yet, it was his unexpected performance that helped Kennedy project among his potential supporters a personal image congruent with the political role he was playing.

Kennedy supporters. The image of Kennedy was transformed from that of an eager, affable, young, and ambitious political aspirant into one that emphasized the competent, dynamic, and quick-thinking candidate.

"His debating techniques showed a quick mind."

"He was alert and interested at all times."

"He seemed to know all the time where to refute Nixon."

"He never fumbled."

"He presented himself as a doer, a leader, a positive thinker."

These are only illustrations of how Kennedy, by his performance, established among potential supporters his character as well as his "right" to the candidacy. Lukewarm supporters became enthusiastic because, as several put it, "People could *see* he was qualified." Said one: "I've switched from an anti-Nixon Democrat to a pro-Kennedy Democrat."

Most of these potential Democrats had expected Kennedy to be "beaten" and, because of this, were prepared to isolate competitive television performance from their consideration of his qualifications for the presidency. At the same time, Nixon's much heralded competence as a performer was a focus for many negative perceptions about his political role. But Nixon's failure to live up to expectations as a performer did not destroy this negative image. The focus on performance also meant that the personal image projected through TV was not likely to gain him trust or to inspire confidence in his qualifications among Democrats. On the contrary, some respondents who had explicitly discounted performance in this regard now went so far as to draw from his "poor" performance conclusions about his fitness. One interpreted "the way he fumbled, ingratiated himself, appeared nervous and not quite rational" to mean that Nixon was "psychologically too upset to be entrusted with the leadership of the country." Observed another, "The poor facial expressions and nervous tension lead me to go so far as to say he looked frightened." The relevance assigned to performance as a measure of the man and the candidate changed among many Democrats.

A poor performance, expected or not, need not result in deterioration of the personal image if it is not linked to political role. Thus six Kennedy supporters, though judging Nixon the poorer performer, emerged with a more positive overall image of Nixon (Table 4). Reading what explanations they could be led to offer for their more charitable view, one discerns that a gnawing distrust of Kennedy led them to question the spontaneity of his performance and to personalize its content. They thus extended sympathy to the apparent victim; yet their electoral choice was not affected, nor did they think less of Kennedy. For example, one housewife (one of the few to anticipate Kennedy's superior performance) explained: "He is a magnetic person, with much polish and a great deal of sex appeal. He'll make a good appearance and will greatly appeal to the younger female voters." Her praise before the debates was thus given grudgingly. She emerged from the first debate unimpressed with "Kennedy's ability to quote figures . . . [since] Kennedy was paying others to get the facts," and she went on to describe how pleased she was that "Nixon gave him a run for his money and didn't take a back seat." She was a regular Democrat, and her vote was not swayed by the increased attraction she felt for Nixon.

Again, one student (a new voter) found Nixon's performance "almost pathetic" and suffered for him. To him Nixon appeared "sometimes pleading, avoiding questions, shocked when attacked, nervous, and anxious, [and] at times I felt very sorry for him." For the first time, the young man said, he had recognized Nixon as a "human being, a complicated personality" rather than a political symbol. This student was one of the few who called the first debate "not quite fair"; he thought newsmen had been "kinder" to Kennedy. But the pro-Republican press, he noted, must have helped "to heal Nixon's wounds" by calling the debate a draw—in the respondent's view Kennedy had clearly won. Performance ultimately moved him from undecided to Kennedy, but after the first debate he described himself as "less in favor of Kennedy than before," even though his overall impression of Kennedy had clearly improved.

Nixon supporters. The Nixon political personality, as already pointed out, was dominated by the perceived political role. Statements by his supporters about the "kind of person Nixon was" were usually formulated in terms of qualifications for office and his ability to perform. An inventory of terms most frequently used before the first debate to describe the personal image included: experienced, competent, better informed than Kennedy, a hard worker, a good American, forceful, honest, sincere, calm, strong, and such phrases as "he can face up to the Russians" and "he can handle Khrushchev." An occasional respondent noted that he was a good family man or had a pleasing personality, and a few attributed the distrust he was known to evoke in others to his "reserve" or "efficiency."

Nixon's performance in the first debate undermined the image of the superior debater most of his supporters had held. The keen disappointment many of them felt was translated into votes for Kennedy only among those few whose choice was founded on rather weak party identification. Most countered Nixon's shaky performance by one or more of three techniques: *isolation, selective perception,* and *personalization.*

Isolation (in the sense of denying the relevance of information to behavioral commitment) has already been noted in the pre-debate responses of Kennedy backers who minimized debating skill as a test of political competence. Now it was the pro-Nixon group who, despite the fact that they had supported evaluations of their candidate by referring to his debating skills, no longer emphasized such skills when his performance proved disappointing.

Selective perception is illustrated by claims that both candidates had been "primed beforehand," an observation often documented by "Kennedy's ability to rattle off figures." Nixon's claim to the presidency was most often justified after the debate by his long advocacy of "sound policies." The candidate's performance was ignored, while the policies he advocated came in for extra attention. By focusing on the political content of Nixon's statements, his supporters, who, presumably, were in agreement with what he believed in, could still define him as the winner, and there was understandably a larger proportion who thought that he had done better or at least as well as Kennedy. Said one, "I think Nixon did better, but of course I'm prejudiced." Others thought that reporters were favoring Kennedy, feeding him easier questions. Kennedy was also accused of having broken the rules by his note-taking and, after the third debate, by reading from notes.[13] Different evaluations of performance thus are a function of elements singled out for attention and of the context in which they are interpreted.

The technique of *personalization* is perhaps a special variant of selective perception. It involves molding essentially ambiguous attributes into an unfavorable personal image of the opposition, and vice versa. For example, one of his supporters remarked on Nixon's "not smiling at all, being ill at ease, and on the defensive," but then went on to interpret this as being "more careful, more subtle, and thinking over a problem." Another woman admitted that "Kennedy came over nicely, if you like his type. He was snide and impolite to make notes while Nixon was speaking." In her final interview, the same woman explained at length that the better the Kennedy performance, the more she came personally to dislike him, while her confidence in Nixon increased; she felt, as she put it, "a real personal contact" with him. Nixon, it was said by another, though a target of Kennedy's "brashness," "never likes to offend anybody." His being "too polite" thus became an explanation of why he failed to live up to expectations.

Personal traits used to explain the performance were

13. Accusations by some Nixon supporters that they had seen Kennedy "cheat" indicate the influence of press reports on what is "seen." After the third debate, Nixon and his spokesmen charged Kennedy with violating an agreement that no notes be used. Kennedy aides denied knowledge of such an agreement and claimed that the controversy concerned only Kennedy's reference to a quotation. In any event, the "cheating" that some viewers had seen could only have been read in the newspaper. There had been no previous public mention of this "rule."

also related to political role. To many, Nixon's hesitations indicated "thoughtfulness" and "cautious modesty," both congruent with the political role a President is expected to play, and thus a favorable contrast to Kennedy's "boasting." As one Nixon supporter put it: "Kennedy always began his statements, '*I* will do this' and '*I* will do that.' Whenever Nixon started to say '*I*,' he checked himself by saying 'the *Republican party* will.' " In another reference Kennedy was seen as "quick-acting, but if he's to talk to Khrushchev, he'd say something he later would regret." Moreover, Nixon, according to some, was not at his best in the first debate because he had recently been hospitalized for an infected knee. He had, however, shown great fortitude: "Nixon could stand up to Kennedy [said one person after the fourth debate]. That shows he could stand up to the Russians."

While Kennedy did improve his overall image among one-third of the Nixon partisans, he improved it largely in terms of "informedness." Thirteen out of thirty Nixon supporters who saw the first debate admitted that Kennedy was better informed than they had thought. But only five out of the same thirty got a more favorable personal image. Many Republicans could only react with hostility on seeing that he was a formidable adversary. It is hardly surprising, therefore, especially in view of the short period covered by the debates, that political preferences should on the whole have remained stable, even though the debates had a definite impact on imagery. What our research did illustrate was a variety of ways in which perceptions were brought into line with electoral choices.

Summary and Implications

Exposure to the televised debates resulted in some rather dramatic changes in candidate image. Voting intentions changed much less, for images were interpreted to serve preference.

In balance, the impact of these debates on the persons studied appears to have favored Kennedy more than Nixon. But when viewed against the backgrounds of voters, the majority of whom had identified themselves with or voted for the Democratic party in the past, Kennedy's gain does not appear to have entailed a large-scale crossing of party lines. Most of the undecided were Democrats-in-conflict, who were won over because Kennedy succeeded in identifying himself with the tradition of the Democratic party.

As the lesser known of the candidates, Kennedy stood a greater chance of being helped by these joint appearances as well as by the campaign generally, an anticipation borne out by this and other research. Still, some of the very elements in the Kennedy performance that worked in his favor among an urban group of viewers such as ours may have produced different responses in other surroundings. For example, note the personal hostility Kennedy's smooth performance aroused among some Nixon voters—in communities where attitudes prevail that were rarely encountered among our sample (such as anti-"big city" or fundamentalist sentiment), the responses may have differed greatly.

Though evidence from our study of the Kennedy-Nixon encounters does not suggest that dramatic and immediate changes in votes can be expected from such TV spectacles in the middle of a campaign, there may nevertheless be important "sleeper" effects that could not be observed by the methods we used. The reactions to the debates were influenced by what viewers remembered about the two performers from past telecasts or (especially in the case of Nixon) as they remembered it from what they read about those telecasts afterward. Efforts to use the debates were revealed in interviews with campaign workers. Among Democrats, the Kennedy performance sparked the organization of viewing groups, generated enthusiasm, and perhaps led to greater campaign efforts, all of which together might have influenced the final vote gains as much as the debates as such.

Nevertheless, the debates marked an important turning point in the campaign. This in itself will make future contestants leery about risking their reputations in open debate with lesser-known challengers. Whether or not an opponent will debate the issues, as well as the conditions for the debate, can become major issues in their own right, and the public is certainly free to draw what conclusions it will from the unwillingness of a candidate to meet his opponent face-to-face. In this connection, the view of Sam Lubell that the most important effect of the debates was to make it "easier for the electorate to accept the election results" [14] must be given serious thought. Kennedy's hairbreadth margin would naturally have been the cause of much bitterness. So would the fear of his Catholicism, which still gripped sizable segments of the American population. Yet, by the time of Kennedy's inauguration, many Nixon backers seemed sufficiently persuaded to give him the benefit of the doubt. Perhaps this would have happened in any event, even without the television performance. Be this as it may, it would seem that the image projected over TV stood Kennedy in good stead as President. By the time he was assassinated just three years later, the positive image he had projected during the debates had been reinforced and converted, in many cases, into potential support for a second term that never came.

14. "Personalities vs. Issues," in Kraus, *The Great Debates,* Chapter 9.

VII

LATE VOTERS AND EARLY RETURNS

The television and radio reporting of the 1964 national election between Lyndon B. Johnson and Senator Barry M. Goldwater made communications history. For the first time, there was the chance that conclusive returns, including projections of the final outcome, would be available to many voters in Western states before they themselves had voted. While as early as 1952 networks used computers to "pick winners," such machines, fascinating as they were to broadcasters and audiences alike, represented novelty or sensation. It was more like a game, with reporters checking to see if the computer predictions came near the mark. By 1964, computer application in this area had reached a new stage of sophistication, and the networks and press associations had finally pooled resources to provide the public with the fastest possible tally of results. The new technology combined with the collaborative effort held a clear prospect that the networks would be able to point to significant trends indicated by bellwether precincts within minutes—and certainly within the hour—after voting ended at 6:30 P.M. in several strategic Eastern states. It would then be just 3:30 P.M. Pacific time. In California, most populous state of the Union, most polling places would remain open till 8:00 P.M.

Throughout the country, but especially in California, citizens were forewarned of possible political effects in the event the networks announced a probable winner early on election night. Newspaper editors and columnists, radio and TV commentators, political candidates and their managers voiced their active concern. Some raised the spectre of vote shifts as returns showed a clear winner. There were allusions to last-minute bandwagon effects benefiting the man shown to be ahead, as well as talk of a large sympathy vote for the apparent underdog. These possibilities were not, however, the chief concern. Anxieties focused particularly on the possibility of a drop in voter turnout in the West, if—as everyone expected—the early returns were to show Johnson with a decisive lead in the East. What concerned people most, then, were reactions to the broadcasts that would produce a "late election day slack."

Candidates and their managers naturally tried to anticipate how such slack might affect their chances for election. For example, the day before the election, Pierre Salinger, the Democratic candidate seeking election to the California Senate seat he held by appointment, took up the issue in a press conference. He was sharply critical of the networks' alleged plans to declare a winner as early as 4:30 P.M. California time. The thousands who might be dissuaded from voting, the senator held, would include more Democrats than Republicans. This would jeopardize his chances in what had been forecast as a close race. In the same vein, Dean Burch, of the Republican National Committee, on the day of the election issued an appeal that networks refrain from early and "unwarranted" interpretations until after polls everywhere had closed.

In the California primary between New York's Governor Rockefeller and Senator Goldwater, held the previous June, a computer-based prediction by Lou Harris had been a near fiasco. At 7:24 P.M., on the basis of very incomplete returns from southern California and thirty-six minutes before polls were to close in the populous San Francisco Bay area of northern California, a center of Rockefeller strength, CBS flatly declared Goldwater the winner, even though at that moment Rockefeller held a lead in the popular vote tally. Goldwater did indeed win but by an extremely narrow margin. Afterward, there were charges, reported by the news media, that persons lined up at northern California polling places, upon hearing this declaration, concluded that the race was over, that their vote no longer mattered, and left without voting. To be sure, these claims remained unconfirmed. Still, they gave rise to the suspicion that the media coverage of the election had been the cause of Rockefeller's defeat.

On election day in 1964, we set out to investigate what effects, if any, the broadcasting of early returns might have on late voters in areas where the polls were still open. The main focus of inquiry was on reactions of persons who learned about the probable outcome before they voted or, in the case of nonvoters, before polls closed and they still had a chance to vote. How did what they heard and saw affect their votes? Were there, as a result, vote switches, vote crystallizations, or abstentions? We also asked how people felt about voting when they already knew the results, how they felt generally about the practice of making predictions from an incomplete tally of votes. Though the research could only document the effects of such broadcasts in *one* election, the study was deliberately designed to throw some light on what might happen under other circumstances in *future* elections. Put another way, this was to be not only a point of departure for isolating factors associated with given effects and determining the likelihood that any given effect would occur, but for considering what long-range implications these broadcasts might have for the political process.

For instance, any effects observed in 1964 might well be, in part, the result of a novel situation, of having conclusive returns available so early on election day. Presumably, in elections to come, people will grow more sophisticated about the fast count and early predictions. But what will such adaptation mean with regard to their feelings about voting or their belief in the legitimacy of the electoral process? Other questions concerned the significance of election night as a unifying experience, during which a national audience holds its breath to learn the outcome and bury the partisan hatchet. Would post-election controversies center on the returns—how they might have influenced the election and how they might be manipulated in the future? The increased speed of communicating results certainly increases the awareness of time differentials between regions, and institutional practices may have to be altered in order to take account of this fact.

To collect data with which we could explore the ramifications of early returns, intensive interviews were held with a sample of 364 registered voters in the East Bay area of California who had not yet gone to the polls by 4 P.M. EST,[1] the time the network election broadcasts were scheduled to start. For purposes of comparison, we also interviewed 116 registered voters in greater Cleveland who, likewise, had not voted by 4 P.M. local

1. The sample was chosen to include voters with a wide variety of different characteristics that might be relevant to an understanding of how they reacted to the broadcasts. The area sample covered Alameda and Contra Costa counties.

time. Since polls in Ohio closed at 6:30 P.M., before the beginning of the election coverage, none of those interviewed there could have received election news from this source.[2]

The methods for selecting respondents from precinct lists were the same in both states. After selecting precincts, we systematically drew names from these lists after removing names of all persons who had already voted by 4 P.M. local time. Interviewing began the day after the election and was completed within eleven days.

What People Knew Before Voting

Events on election day 1964 clearly corroborated the expectation that an early winner would be declared from very incomplete returns. Explicit projections of a Johnson victory by the three major networks came at 3:48 P.M., at 4:43 P.M., and at 4:50 P.M PST, while voting in California and other neighboring states was still in progress. In the California precincts we studied, three out of five registered voters who had not yet gone to the polls by 4 P.M. local time had heard something about how the race for President was going by the time they did go or, if they were nonvoters, before the polls closed (see Table 1). The news available to many of these

2. The early poll-closing time in Ohio turned out to be an advantage. Regular network news programs heard at 6:30 P.M. Eastern time actually contained significant news of election trends, even though they were not formally a part of the election coverage.

Table 1 Election News Heard Before Voting

	California (N=364)	Ohio (N=116)
Heard Something	61%	14%
Heard Nothing	37%	85%
No Answer	2%	1%
	100%	100%

people was quite definitive. Over half of those who, before voting, were exposed to some election news (or one out of three persons interviewed), concluded from what they heard that a Johnson victory was certain and that the race for President was, for all practical purposes, already decided. Only six persons (less than 2 per cent of the total sample) heard some election news before they voted that gave them the impression Goldwater was making a comparatively strong showing (Table 2).

Table 2 Conclusion Drawn from Election News Heard Before Voting

	California (N=220)	Ohio (N=16)
Johnson "Had Won," Certain to Win	56%	56%
Johnson Ahead, Will Probably Win	16%	25%
No Conclusion, "Too Early"	25%	19%
Goldwater Ahead or Doing Well	3%	0%
	100%	100%

The two broadcast media were, beyond doubt, the chief source of early election news; radio and TV were mentioned as their primary source of information by 81 per cent of those who had heard something by the time they voted. More people mentioned radio than television, probably because so many tuned in as they drove home from work or to the polls. Yet, television was clearly the more effective of the two in giving people a clear idea of the likely outcome. This effectiveness does not appear to be so much an attribute of the medium as of media use. In contrast to radio listening, television viewing was more likely to occur after work, when the returns coming in were more definitive and viewers could give them their undivided attention. That the network coverage provided a fairly clear indication of the impending Johnson victory from the minute it went on the air can be surmised from the fact that 71 per cent who first started to follow these returns from 4 P.M. PST on said that, as soon as they had turned on their set, they knew "right away" that the race was more or less decided. This proportion increased to near 90 per cent among persons who first tuned in at a later hour. The 15 per cent who received whatever pre-voting information they had from "other people" were probably hearing secondhand what originally came over radio or television.

It must nevertheless be emphasized that not all the information with which California late voters went to the polls, and which was available also to nonvoters while they could still vote, came from the network election coverage that began at 4 P.M. Even in Ohio, where polls had closed before these broadcasts could be heard, one out of seven interviewees claimed he had had some news while still free to make a decision, and a few even said they had become certain of the impending Johnson landslide before voting. There had been news bulletins on radio and television and scattered returns in Cleveland's afternoon paper. These same reports had been heard even earlier in their day by Californians. By the time polls closed in California, there were newspaper and radio reports on voting trends in *all* sections of the country.

Nor did viewers or listeners in California who had become certain the election was decided necessarily reach this conclusion after hearing computer-based predictions. A person who heard such a prediction was more likely to be certain about the outcome than others who did not, but by far the largest number of those "certain" before they voted said the trend was evident from the tally of the popular vote.

Comparing conclusions reached by three groups of voters helps pin down this impact of the early election network coverage. Among California late voters who had:

followed network returns before voting, 56 per cent became "certain" that Johnson had won;

not followed network returns before voting, 20 per cent became "certain."

Of Ohio late voters, 14 per cent became "certain." The last group, especially, could only have had the scantiest information on election trends. If they reached a certain conclusion, it was because, as some volunteered, the news only confirmed what they had "known" all along.

These observations show that conclusions drawn from the news available did not depend solely on news content but also on what people had expected beforehand. Thus, it obviously took more convincing information to invalidate an expectation that Goldwater would win than to confirm one about a Johnson landslide. Those who had anticipated a landslide became certain of the outcome, before voting, about twice as often (42 per cent) as those who had given Goldwater a near-even or better chance to win (22 per cent). Political preference, by contrast, made little difference: Goldwater supporters were as likely as Johnson supporters to accept the "unpleasant fact" of a Johnson victory.

The Broadcasts and Voter Turnout

How much late election day slack could be traced to the special network broadcasts? Interviews with these 364 Californians, all of them registered voters, had as their payoff just one single case of late election day slack in response to the broadcasts: an angry Goldwater enthusiast who became so dismayed at the news of the lopsided Johnson margin that he simply gave up and did not vote, even though he said he had never given Goldwater much chance to win in the first place.

A single case hardly provides a sound basis for quantitative generalization. Still, one of the most startling and unexpected findings of our study was the low rate of nonvoting among registered voters.[3] We simply could not find many nonvoters, despite the fact that our California sample was so drawn that it should have yielded interviews with at least one nonvoter for every three late voters. The total yield of nonvoters was only twelve. The situation in Ohio was similar.

This lack of nonvoters seemed explicable in one or both of two ways: either (1) our techniques were at fault in that nonvoters were somehow evading our interviewers or falsely stating that they had voted, or (2) the precinct lists from which we sampled were in some way inaccurate and greatly exaggerated the actual amount of nonvoting. We accordingly decided to check on alleged nonvoters. In California, precinct sign-in rosters were compared with registration lists, yielding a list of 351 persons who were officially registered but had not voted.[4] Selected interviewers were instructed to contact these nonvoters and determine whether they had in fact voted, and if they were unable to contact them, to determine why they were so hard to reach.

It shortly became apparent that a considerable number of our official nonvoters in California were in fact "spurious" nonvoters. Seventy-one per cent of the "nonvoters" in California and 59 per cent in Ohio had either

3. H. Mendelsohn and D. Fuchs report similar observations. See their articles in *Public Opinion Quarterly,* xxx (Summer, 1966).

4. Of these, 234 had been drawn in our original sample.

moved out of the precinct or had died. For people in this group, the "nonvoter" label was a mere artifact of their names still appearing on the lists of precincts in which they no longer lived.

On the basis of official registration records in the California precincts, the nonvoting rate would have been 14 per cent; it would have been 16 per cent in Ohio. We tried to correct for this inflation of the number of nonvoters with the utmost conservatism, subtracting from the group of alleged nonvoters only those who were stated by family or neighbors to have died or moved out of the precinct. For one reason or another, no information could be obtained for 15 per cent of the alleged nonvoters in California (and 19 per cent in Ohio). Still, when so corrected, the proportion of nonvoters in California dropped to 4 per cent and the proportion in Ohio to 7 per cent. Thus, relative to Ohio, nonvoting in California appeared even lower than it did before. The 4 per cent nonvoting rate in California accordingly represents the maximum number within which broadcast-induced late election slack could have occurred. That is to say, if *every* registrant who did not vote had heard network returns before polls closed and thereby decided not to cast a vote, a maximum of 4 per cent of the electorate could have been so affected.

Much of the verified nonvoting in both states was due either to illness or to unavoidable and unanticipated absence out of town on election day. Hence, this logical —but obviously improbable—upper limit must be further reduced by at least the number who were physically unable to vote. Among those remaining—perhaps 2.5 per cent of all registered voters—lack of political interest was clearly the most important reason for failure to appear at the polls.

Table 3 ***Nonvoting Among Registered Voters in California and Ohio***

	California	Ohio
Percentage Who Failed to Vote	14	16
Percentage of "Nonvoters" Who Moved or Died	71	59
Corrected Actual Percentage of Nonvoters	4	7

Was nonvoting in California more frequent among Republican or Democratic registrants? According to official registration records from these precincts, Democrats appeared to be in the majority among those who stayed at home, but when the estimate was based on corrected rates, it pointed to a slight excess of Republican nonvoters. Given the importance of factors in nonvoting other than the returns, there is no reason to suspect that this slight excess was a result of the broadcasts.

When we focused directly on the impact of network broadcasts, their subordinate importance as a cause of slack became still clearer. Nonvoters, compared to late voters, had less interest and were less involved in the election campaign. Fewer of them followed returns before the polls closed. The same characteristics that account for the lower rate of exposure among nonvoters also lower the probability that they will vote. Among the total sample, we found nobody who had deliberately delayed his vote until he could first learn how things were going.

Vote Decisions: Crystallizations and Switches

We also investigated the other possibility—that the election broadcasts encouraged vote switching and helped crystallize the votes of persons who otherwise might not have voted. With this possibility in mind, we asked every voter to tell us about any political decisions he had made on election day. We asked about this before the questioning turned to the effect of the broadcasts.

Both in California and Ohio, most election day decisions that were mentioned had to do with voting on candidates for lower offices or on some proposition before the voters. An identical 2 per cent of late voters in each state reported a decision affecting their vote for President. All of these involved a vote crystallization, rather than a switch, by a person who, after some prior doubts, had finally come to a firm decision. But these decisions were not evenly distributed between the two candidates. Of the seven crystallizations in California, five resulted in Goldwater votes, one in a vote for Johnson, and the seventh refused to tell how he had cast his ballot for President. Of two crystallizations in Ohio, one was for Goldwater, the other for Johnson.

The natural question is whether the apparent preponderance of last-minute shifts toward Goldwater reflected the influence of early returns or whether these crystallizations would have occurred in any event. The evidence suggests that the sharp conflict within the Republican party had subjected many Republicans to cross-pressures and delayed the crystallization of their votes. The majority of these last-minute crystallizations came from anti-Goldwater Republicans who hitherto could not see themselves voting for Johnson. Crystallizations in Ohio, obviously, could not be attributed to the election broadcasts. But even in California, no cause-effect relationship could be established. In fact, the last-minute crystallizers there had less often become "certain" of the outcome than other late voters.

When we looked at the process of vote crystallization, it became quite evident that the mere approach of a moment for decision forces the voter to make a choice. Thus, nearly one out of five late voters in California—compared with one out of six in Ohio—reported that he had "seriously considered" at some time during the campaign not voting at all, or voting but not voting for President or senator. All but a few had resolved these doubts before election day. Three late voters in California and two in Ohio actually cast ballots without voting for President. The number who voted but passed up the opportunity to vote for United States senator was larger. Obviously, the presidential contest plays a central role in getting out the vote, and anyone inclined to cast a ballot could not, without some unease, refrain from voting for the highest office.

Attitudinal Reactions

Feelings about and attitudes toward the election broadcasts were far more pervasive in 1964 than the small number of overt reactions would suggest. Among persons who had heard some election news while they could still make a vote decision, the large majority—72 per cent to be exact—did say, when specifically asked about this, that the information had made them neither more nor less eager to vote. If it did make a difference, however, the person was more likely to respond by becoming more eager to vote. Positive reactions outnumbered negative reactions by a better than 3 to 2 ratio.

Why should anyone, upon hearing that the outcome of an election could not possibly be overturned by votes yet to be cast, become *more* eager to vote? Why did those who felt *less* like voting because of what they heard go ahead and vote anyway? Even though these reactions were rarely translated into changes in overt behavior, they help explain the prevalence of stability over change while pointing to the kinds of circumstances under which such covert tendencies might pass the threshold of action. Turning to attitudinal responses, we shall try to pin down the role the early election broadcasts played in 1964.

To begin with, whether a person experienced any

change of attitude depended upon the conclusion he drew from whatever news he heard. The more certain a person was of his conclusion, the more likely he was to have some kind of reaction and to become less eager to vote. In other words, some voters did react with feelings of futility to the news that Johnson had already won.

Second, voters who concluded that the election was not going as they had expected reacted even more strongly. Those who, before the election, had not believed that Johnson would win by a landslide, or even that he would win, and then saw a runaway victory materialize before their eyes, tended also to become "less eager" to vote.

Finally, underdog perceptions (Goldwater supporters seeing their candidate was losing) elicited more reactions one way or the other than bandwagon perceptions (Johnson supporters finding that Johnson had won or was about to win), and the latter, in turn, elicited more reactions than perceptions about the outcome that were entirely inconclusive.

In contrast to these responses to rather conclusive presidential returns, the very scattered and partial returns from the California Senate race, available to a few who voted very late in the day, had a decidedly positive effect on the eagerness to vote. These "more eager" reactions were concentrated among Salinger supporters who found the man they expected to win was trailing. These underdog perceptions, coming at a time when the outcome of that contest was still very much in doubt, appear to have had a definite mobilizing effect.

Also, some late voters, explaining their reaction to presidential returns, mentioned the Senate race. Several evidently heeded Salinger's advance warning not to be dissuaded from voting should early returns show a Johnson landslide. But the news that Johnson had won was more likely to make the person anticipating an "extremely close" Senate race more eager to vote, whether he was for or against Johnson. In any case, the trend of the senatorial contest evidently helped forestall any slack that might have followed news that the presidential contest was all but over.

The Law of Minimal Consequences

Why was the overall effect of the broadcast returns on the behavior of voters so minimal? In explanation, we point to factors and conditions, some general and some specific to the 1964 election, that made it difficult for the election broadcasts to change voting intentions. The fact that very few specific consequences could be observed in the short run does not, however, preclude the possibility of more important effects in other elections or over the long run.

The minimal impact of the returns came from three sources: (1) the smallness of the group potentially open to influences, (2) the neutralization of any impetus toward change by countervailing influences, and (3) the stability of attitudes that support voting and the different specific cognitions with which these attitudes are compatible.

The susceptible group. To be susceptible to any influence on election day, a person had to be registered in advance, defer voting until after significant returns began coming in, tune in on the election coverage or talk with someone who did, and then find his expectations—on which his vote intention was based—invalidated. Mere confirmation, from returns heard before voting, of what a person already believed in the offing was unlikely to dissuade him from what he intended to do.

According to best estimates, some two-thirds of all California citizens of voting age were registered in 1964. Between 25 and 30 per cent on the lists from which the California sample was drawn had not voted by 4 P.M. local time; of those interviewed, 40 per cent were found to have been following election returns prior to voting, and the proportion who had heard at least some election news was even larger. These figures reached staggering proportions among those who went to the polls in the hour before closing time. But despite the large number who had heard something about the outcome of the race before the polls closed, only 12 per cent of the late voters and nonvoters studied said their expectations were invalidated. Most respondents said they had never expected anything but a Johnson victory by at least a comfortable margin.

Moreover, prior research findings would indicate that

persons most open to influence are those least interested in the campaign and with the least partisan involvement. Many of these never register in the first place and are, for this reason, beyond the range of possible influence from any returns. Among registrants it was the less politically interested, involved, and politically sophisticated person who, before the election, believed that Goldwater's chances were pretty good. But the less politically interested, involved, and sophisticated a person, the less likely he was to hear something about the race or follow network returns before he voted. Hence, a large proportion of the relatively few people whose expectations might have been invalidated before they voted were exposed to early returns only casually, or not at all, and so were not open to influence. As for the rest, the election returns did not contradict what they expected. That the election returns should have shocked so few people indicates that any bandwagon or underdog psychology at work had already had its effects on people before election day.

What a person had heard by the time he went to the polls was largely a matter of when he voted. The question is: Did certain types of voters wait to vote until the returns were "in"? Our study revealed that voters who showed up during the last ninety minutes before the polls closed were not an exceptionally volatile group, pushed into voting by a last-minute electioneering drive. On the contrary, the "late late voters" included a rather large number of the better-educated and politically sophisticated "independents," particularly Republicans-in-conflict insofar as the 1964 election was concerned. The votes of these persons reflected much deliberation, while their concern, like that of many others, extended to races other than that for the top office. Therefore, casting a vote still made sense to them, even though the presidential race, so it seemed, had been irrevocably decided by the votes already cast.

Countervailing influences. The reports reaching voters on election day were viewed by them within a context of prior and competing communications. Among these, of course, were urgings to Goldwaterites that they vote early to avoid the possibility of influence, and the warning Salinger issued to his followers not to be lulled into complacency by an apparent Democratic tide. At the same time, the nonpartisan saturation campaign to get out the vote continued right through election day and inundated voters from every side—from the mass media, from election workers, and from friends and associates.

Many respondents reported that they themselves, on election day, had urged others to be sure to vote or had themselves been so urged by others. Reports of partisan attempts to switch votes by political argument were far fewer in number. Only twelve persons, all of whom voted, indicated either that they had been the target of a suggestion that it no longer made much difference whether or not they voted, or that they had voiced this feeling to others. Though all of these manifest dissuasion attempts referred to election trends, they were made in a semi-serious fashion in conversations that only helped to focus attention on the election, contribute to the excitement, and emphasize that voting was the order of business for this day.

The motivation to vote. Casting a ballot can have different subjective significance for different voters. We found that the way voters respond to returns broadcast before they have voted depends a good deal on which of three different orientations to voting motivates them. Thus, the widespread expectation that news of a Johnson landslide would cause slack was based on an image of a voter motivated primarily by the *utility* he believes his ballot to have. This utility depends on the capacity of his vote to influence the outcome. Once an election appears "decided," voting assumedly loses its utility. It no longer makes any difference whether or not one votes, and the voter may be dissuaded from going to the polls.

A voter's *partisan involvement,* a second kind of orientation, contributes to the stability of reactions in a situation such as that just described. Where the vote serves primarily as an ideological expression, as a declaration of solidarity, it is to that extent independent of immediate practical consideration but serves as a testament of ideological preference. More than that, the belief that one's vote has utility, when perceived within a context of partisan involvement, can be maintained even after one or the other candidate appears clearly to have won. Voters with such a partisan perspective usually assess the implications of particular returns for the outcome of other races and for future elections. Such a perspective, as we have seen, led some voters to assess the possible effect of news about the presidential race on the outcome of the Senate election. Others voted, no doubt, because they wanted to hold down the Johnson margin; some, to repudiate the Goldwater brand of Republicanism so unambiguously that it would no longer be a political force.

Stability in electoral participation is further supported by a third orientation, one that neither takes account of the utility of the vote nor has anything to do with partisanship. Many people look upon voting as an *obligation of citizenship,* as a "God-given right," as one California voter put it. In this respect, casting a ballot is a testimonial of a person's commitment to the democratic process. Even where there is no electoral contest, many ballots are cast simply as an expressive gesture. Tabulations, not shown here, indicated that persons who saw in the vote the "only way" of influencing government officials, who had a good deal of confidence in their own political know-how, and who were primarily voting "for" (rather than "against") a candidate tended, by and large, to become "more eager" to vote after hearing returns, whether or not they perceived any utility in their vote or were, as partisans, highly involved.

To understand, then, why there was so little slack and why, on the contrary, votes continued to crystallize on election day, one must consider not only whether the votes still to be cast had practical utility but also to what extent they expressed partisan and nonrational commitments.

Implications

It is apparent that those susceptible to influence constituted a limited group to begin with, and that what returns a person heard were perceived within a framework of an individual's expectations of the outcome and the meaning he attached to his vote. A variety of such factors generally limits the short-run conversion potential of mass media content.[5] Therefore, underlying the whole relationship between the election night broadcasts and their effects on late voters is the "law of minimal consequences."[6] Short-term effects in the 1964 election were certainly limited. Yet insofar as the above law represents only a probability statement, the question arises whether the same conditions that caused limited impact will also prevail in other elections. Also, this law applies only to effects over the short run. May there not be long-range effects of early broadcasts that have not yet been felt? In other words, how much can one generalize about impact from a case study of a single election in which the fast count and early declaration of a winner were still novelties?

Impact in other elections. The impact of early re-

5. Klapper, *The Effects of Mass Communication.*
6. A term coined by Hope L. Klapper of New York University.

turns in the 1964 presidential election was related, first, to the content of *pre-voting perceptions* and to the specific conclusions people drew from them. Second, individual reactions to these perceptions differed, depending on whether what was heard merely confirmed what was expected or invalidated it. *Prior estimates* were therefore another important mediating factor. Third, voters differed with regard to interest, involvement, and sophistication. These *characteristics of the electorate* meant that not all registered voters were equally susceptible to influence from early returns. Fourth, the specific *choices before the electorate* affected the relative strengths of the several motivations for voting.

The 1964 election obviously differed from most other elections in two respects: the unambiguous way in which early returns foretold the final result, and the high proportion of late voters for whom this merely confirmed exactly what they had expected. These two factors work in opposite directions. On the one hand, the near certainty of information in the early returns made it difficult for voters to maintain contrary beliefs, or withhold judgments, by focusing selectively on some items of information while ignoring the apparent trend. On the other hand, most forecasts before the election had been so one-sided in their indication of an easy Johnson victory that very few people experienced the election news as any kind of surprise.

The California Senate election between Murphy and Salinger, held concurrently with the presidential election, presents quite a different picture. Pre-voting perceptions of the likely outcome were quite ambiguous, for only very few districts had reported by the time polls closed; and this inconclusiveness was reinforced by pre-election forecasts of an extremely close race unlikely to be decided early in the evening. Under these circumstances, early and ambiguous returns had a definite mobilizing influence.

There are only a limited number of combinations between pre-election forecasts and network predictions based upon early returns. The following diagram sets them forth schematically:

Indication of the Outcome in Early Returns	Pre-Election Forecasts	
	One-Sided Race	Close Race
Conclusive: Outcome "Decided"	1. Confirmation 2. Upset	3. Resolution of Doubts
Ambiguous: Outcome Still "In Doubt"	4. Selective Interpretations	5. Confirmation of Doubts

The key word in each box describes the predominant type of response for each combination.

Types 1 and 5 both refer to conditions under which

the invalidation of prior expectations will be rare and the impetus toward slack from this source greatly reduced. But the confirmation in these two types of elections is apt to have rather different consequences. The Type 1 election would elicit relatively mild reactions, because voters would already have oriented themselves to the outcome indicated by the early returns. By contrast, a confirmation of doubts in the Type 5 election, through the apparent but unconfirmed indication of a close race, would probably exert a strong mobilizing influence on the electorate. The longer the appearance of a see-saw battle can be maintained, the more will the early returns exert an impetus toward voting.

The "ambiguity" in the returns can be of two distinct types. On the one hand, ambiguity in the returns may be due to the small number of districts reporting, to contradictions between what the tally of the popular vote appears to show and the explicit prediction of a network (as in the 1964 California primary), or to contradictory interpretations between individuals on the same network or between two networks. On the other hand, a race so close that no one can predict the outcome with any confidence results in ambiguous returns of quite a different kind. Returns ambiguous in the first sense (only a few districts reporting) are illustrated by the Type 4 election. Their direct impact would be greatly reduced because conclusions drawn in these circumstances are influenced by what viewers expect. Both positive and negative reactions would be few in number. Selective perceptions would also influence the conclusions drawn in the Type 5 election, where returns indicate a close race. But the stirring of hopes and the confirmation of fears should result in some mobilization of support.

The potential for slack is probably greatest in the Type 2 and Type 3 elections, because here the returns bring about a definite change in the definition of the outcome. Expectations may be upset, but disappointed followers can do nothing about it. Both types involve invalidations: in the one case, the expected winner loses; in the other, a close race turns into a clear-cut victory. To be sure, our analysis of reactions to returns in 1964—a Type 1 election—did not discriminate between these two kinds of invalidation, i.e., those who had expected the election to be "extremely close" and then had their doubts "resolved" by the returns, versus those for whom the returns were an "upset." Both groups appeared to have reacted in essentially the same way, and we had too few cases of either type of invalidation to be able to make any fine distinctions.

Under what conditions may broadcast predictions become either self-fulfilling or self-defeating? One must take a number of factors into account. Although changes in voting behavior tend, as we pointed out, to be infrequent, in a closely contested election even a minuscule percentage of the total vote could overturn the result. Yet, in that close a contest it is unlikely that early returns would lend themselves to any clear prediction, and networks are increasingly reluctant to go out on a limb early on election night. On the other hand, the earlier a network can predict with confidence the outcome from a minute proportion of the vote, and the more broadcast predictions of this sort find public acceptance, the greater will be their potential impact on voting behavior.

The close connection between pre-voting perceptions and pre-election forecasts suggests that the improvement of polling techniques will reduce the likelihood of Type 2 elections in which expectations are upset. Wider dissemination of polling results leads to greater uniformity in individual expectations, based as they are on more nearly identical sources of information. The self-appointed expert with his "ear close to the ground" is disappearing, and the projective element in popular estimates—whereby supporters overestimate their candidate's chances—is likewise on the wane. These trends are balanced in part by the extreme caution with which pollsters now avoid flat predictions. Since the fiasco of 1948, when most polls wrongly forecast that Truman would lose, pollsters have hedged their estimates in every conceivable way. If this continues, the Type 3 situation—where the "close" race turns out not to be so "close"—will occur with greater frequency.

Many late voters voiced the belief that pre-election polls influenced the outcome in 1964. Whatever the validity of charges that polls adversely affected Goldwater's chances, on the assumption that "nobody wants to vote for a loser," these polls did have an indirect influence on the response to the election broadcasts.

Because the forecasts of a completely one-sided race were so fully confirmed even by the earliest returns, they helped immunize voters against the possibility of an invalidation. Only if the polls should suffer another fiasco, comparable to the one in 1948, will returns upset the expectations of many voters.

Nevertheless, there will always be voters whose own expectations differ from those disseminated by the mass media. Mavericks, whose expectations are invalidated by returns, will thus be found in every election. To the extent that these persons respond to information by deviating from their prior intentions, this group is always a source of potential instability. At the same time, to the extent that this group is also less informed, because it is less involved, and therefore less apt to pay attention to or draw conclusions from early returns, the potential number of changes is limited.

The impact of certainty and of invalidations would be least in elections in which voter interest is widely dispersed among many electoral contests instead of being focused on a single race or referendum. In 1964, balloting going on concurrently for other offices and for propositions inhibited the slack effect. Logically, all other things being equal, the danger of slack resulting from broadcast returns is greatest in areas of one-party dominance (inasmuch as other races are unlikely to be affected by any decrease in the vote for President); in party primaries where the contest is only for a single office; in special by-elections; or where a referendum is called to resolve some particular issue.

These types of contests have in common still another feature: a lower and generally more variable voting turnout. The efficacy of the last-minute effort to bring out the vote, as well as the possibility of slack, are increased by the large number of registered voters who are only marginally committed to voting. Highly variable social psychological influences are likely to have a greater influence on whether or not these persons will vote. The electorate in a national election apparently does not have this character. Those who vote are strongly committed toward voting, and most nonvoting, as we have seen, results from institutional and physical obstacles. The easing of registration requirements or the adoption of some procedure for "automatic" registration could swell the number of marginally committed voters in a national election and so contribute to potential instability.

Long-range and ancillary effects. Any innovation in communications—whether the admission of the press to legislative debates, the broadcasting of political party conventions, the televising of presidential press conferences, and so forth—has invariably evoked alarm. Some change always accompanies its introduction, but the potential danger to political institutions is, in retrospect, almost always found to have been exaggerated. The process by which individuals react and the ramifications of their reactions for the workings of institutions are always more complex, and hence the effects far more subtle, than the alarmists can anticipate. Indeed, the high-pitched sense of alarm may itself be one of the firmest guarantees against sudden change.

Long-term adaptation to the fast tabulation of votes and computer-based predictions involves learning how to live with them. For the individual voter, this means learning to evaluate the meaning of any apparent trend or explicit prediction. Will repeated experience with computer-dominated election night reports increase or decrease any susceptibility to influence? The answer depends on many things, including whether trust in the returns (and their accuracy) grows or declines. It depends also on the amount of critical reserve among the audience and on the tendency to vote early or to avoid pre-voting exposure to returns.

To begin with, the accuracy of early predictions of electoral trends will have something to do with the credibility they will enjoy. Performance, so far, has been pretty mixed. For example, in 1960, one network first called the election for Richard Nixon but quickly modified this prediction as soon as sizable returns began to come in. Again, in the June California primary preceding the 1964 election, an early prediction by pollster Lou Harris, vividly remembered by many voters there, nearly redounded to the discredit of the network concerned: the narrow margin by which the prediction was vindicated in the final returns helped feed the subsequent controversy over broadcast-induced effects.

Past mistakes have evidently made broadcasters more cautious. They have become increasingly careful to explain the basis on which predictions are made and to hedge their predictions with semantic qualifications—"probable winners," "indicated winners," "declared winners," and so on. In state and local reports since 1964, some predictions have turned out to be incorrect. Yet there was little embarrassment or public outcry. The broadcasters had made allowance for such possibilities from the start of their programs.

The more "experienced" viewers among the election night audience, we found, were not only more knowledgeable about how predictions are made long before all votes are in but also had more faith in their accuracy. It would seem likely that as more voters come to understand the distinction between the tally of the vote and the projection of trends from sample districts, more will also recognize that broadcasters are simply applying a new technology to improve their interpretations of trends in the returns. Elections have almost always been called before the final vote was tallied. Only the practice of declaring a winner before the final vote is cast represents a departure.

If trust in the reliability of early predictions is likely to increase as they gain in accuracy, there is still the question of how voters will act to avoid being influenced. Voters in Western states are by now keenly aware that they are special targets of influence. If news media persist in broadcasting returns before polls are closed, individuals and groups will adapt to the speed-up in returns. People obviously can deliberately vote before returns become available; they can avoid hearing news;

they can persuade themselves in advance of the importance of the margin of victory or of the other races. Their awareness is bound to increase. This, coupled with the exercise of responsible caution by broadcasters, should minimize the influence of exposure to returns on voting behavior.

Still, the fact that the net balance of vote changes had no effect on the outcome of the election in 1964 does not mean that the broadcast of returns before polls closed had no effect upon voters, or that there will be no effects in the future. While respondents did not change their intention to vote (or not to vote) as a result of their exposure to news before voting, many did say that casting a vote knowing the election was over amounted to a partial disfranchisement. It seemed to them that their ballots counted for less.

Interest in an early prediction appears to have been stronger among late voters in Ohio, where 25 per cent chose this as one of their reasons for selecting a particular television channel after they had voted, than in California, where this reason was chosen by only 11 per cent. Apparently, Easterners like to know the outcome of an election without having to stay up most of the night, whereas Californians could count on hearing significant results rather early in the evening. Yet, sizable minorities both in California (45 per cent) and in Ohio (38 per cent) agreed with the statement, "Being told who the winner will be early in the evening, before most votes have actually been counted, takes the fun out of election night broadcasts."

Even when knowing the likely outcome before voting does not contribute to a sense of disfranchisement, it can make it more difficult to vote out of a simple sense of obligation. It is altogether possible that voters in areas where early returns are available long before polls close will learn to take a careful estimate of the utility of their ballot before they cast it. Imagine, for instance, a very close election in which early returns indicate that California—or Oregon or Hawaii or Alaska—would supply the electoral votes necessary for victory. With the electoral votes in other states already accounted for, attention would turn to the West and what voters there would do. If the expectation of a close race had been widespread, and if many people were undecided about whether to vote or for whom to vote, large numbers of people might delay going to the polls until they had first heard how the election was going. The fact that few voters waited around in 1964 does not mean that more may not do so in some future election.

There are circumstances under which having a good idea of how the race was going could, conceivably, alter the general tendency not to vote for a third party in presidential elections. Under a two-party system, the necessity for electoral coalitions presents a formidable barrier in the way of third-party protest. Especially people who feel they are voting for the lesser of two evils will be disinclined to defect to a minor party for fear of bringing the greater evil to power. Early returns will improve their knowledge of what the odds are.

There is in this not so much the possibility that an election would be won or lost through the influence of returns as that new considerations might enter the electoral choice. Voters would no longer cast ballots as a simple expression of their preferences. Instead, they would be encouraged to use a rational strategy, based on whatever information they had from polls and returns.

Most of the outcry against the early returns centered on the disfranchisement of the late voter in the West. It is equally possible to look upon him as unfairly "advantaged" because he is in a position to see the consequence of his vote and to capitalize on this knowledge. In no sense, however, is this a re-creation of a town meeting, where the roll is called and everyone can see how the vote is about to go. In such a situation persons can "pass" in order to cast their vote later at a more crucial time; they can, for that matter, reverse their vote if, given the existing division, they come to find it advisable to do so. But in a national election, by contrast, a ballot is irrevocably cast. Although individual ballots are secret, those voting late have more opportunity to base their own vote on estimates of political trends. They may be the only ones to vote knowing that a decision has already been made. Theoretically, the canons of courtesy that enjoin a loser to concede—even long before the tally has been completed—as soon as the trend is unmistakable could produce a concession even while balloting was still in progress. What would the voter do then?

It is to reduce disparities in the access to knowledge that the press everywhere has usually insisted on unrestricted publicity. In raising these possibilities, we mean to indicate that there may be other unanticipated consequences. The vote count has an important place in political life in the United States. New ways of reporting elections are bound, over the long run, to alter the election night ritual. To stay up on election night to learn who the new President will be has been, especially since the advent of radio, an opportunity to participate in a national event. A near-majority of Californians, as pointed out, responded to a query about whether the fun had gone out of election night by saying the experience was not the same. Election night has been a unifying experience containing elements of the "sacred." When, in addition, issues are raised about how many votes might have been changed or races determined as a consequence of the broadcasts, the returns become linked to the divisive controversies inevitably aroused by any electoral campaign. The possible consequences for political behavior are difficult to anticipate.

Technological innovations, by their nature, call for new sets of rules to cope with their effects. Certainly, the new technology for data processing and quick dissemination makes it possible to have more reliable forecasts faster, and even before the election. Many voters have a keen interest in learning the outcome of an election as soon as this information becomes available, and competition among the news media will make voluntary restraints difficult to enforce. As is now the case with pre-election polls, political managers are constantly tempted to leak to the public results which they judge will redound to their interest. Unless there is a complete blackout of broadcasts, the normal flow of news will not cease, but there will be less of a check on its reliability. Surely, full coverage by a professionally competent and responsible staff is preferable to news leaks designed to advance partisan interests. Any measure that curtailed the right of news gathering agencies to check up on returns or to disseminate them to some areas would indeed represent an interference with the right of the public to know.

The proposal for a uniform polling day, suggested publicly by Dr. Frank Stanton, with balloting all over the country ending at the same hour, would permit the fullest exploitation of the new technology. Results from all parts of the country would be available at about the same time, so that all suspicion about the influence of early returns would be eliminated. Indeed, there would be no "early returns." The quick answers provided could contribute to a feeling that people all over the country were sharing in a simultaneous experience. The fun and excitement of the long vigil into election night would be abbreviated, but it would no doubt be replaced by a new ritual of interpretation in depth of the returns (what groups and sections voted which way) and a new ritual of concession and victory statements. Perhaps more attention would be given to state and local contests.

The justification for new election regulations does not reside in the demonstration of direct effects. But given the power inherent in the new communications technology, setting rules to maintain "equality" seems preferable to depending on self-immunization by individual voters or trusting that politicians will employ strategies to neutralize the advantage one or the other side might enjoy were early returns to continue to be broadcast.

VIII

THE QUESTION OF ACTUALITY

"Television as a news medium," David Karp wrote twenty years after its debut, "has acquired a peculiar and powerful status that no other medium has ever held. Marshall McLuhan . . . has, in fact, classified television's on-the-spot 'actuality' reporting of events as-they-happen as a totally new form of communication [that] has transformed the 'mere' reader into an electronic participant. The viewer is turned on to what is really happening as if he had an electrical umbilicus tied to the tube. In McLuhan's view, the television watcher has finally achieved the status of Aldous Huxley's 'feelie' participant, and damned high time it happened, too." [1]

Some years ago we participated in a seminar on public communication at Columbia University, where mass-communications researchers told McLuhan that the findings just didn't bear out the message he was receiving. Nor, for that matter, do our own studies discussed in this book. Rather, they show that television, as well as radio and print, always introduces some element of refraction into the actuality it conveys. Television has its own special biases; and "electronic participation" is something clearly different from direct participation. If television has acquired a special and powerful status as a news medium, the reason may lie less in the qualities its heralds proclaim than in the readiness of reporters, politicians, and the public to believe in its actuality and its ability to reveal the truth. It is almost a truism, to paraphrase the words of the sociologist W. I. Thomas, that "since people define certain qualities of TV as real, they are real in their consequences for political life." What are the reality and the consequences of television as a news medium?

1. *New York Times Magazine,* November 19, 1967, p. 143.

Refraction and the Mass Media

The continuing revolution in communication that began with the distribution of cheap print has made it possible for more and more people to live more of their lives "at a distance." They have the opportunity to participate in the political, cultural, and intellectual life of far-off places which they know because of the media of mass communication. The larger world is brought into villages through radio and into urban homes through television. As this happens, people naturally become more responsive to events, objects, and personalities outside the range of their immediate experience. More and more they are asked to empathize with strangers in strange surroundings.

But these developments, which broaden people's vision, are not without paradox. The paradox results from the *separation* of experience and participation, both of which had previously been linked. As the media bring the world closer, the more intimate "acquaintance with"—the product of direct involvement—is replaced by a more superficial "knowledge about" a great many more events and personalities. This knowledge is mediated, that is, in compressing space and time and eliminating physical barriers, the mass media invariably introduce some distortion into "actuality."

We do not imply that the media characteristically and deliberately manipulate reports of distant events.

This is certainly *not* the case. By and large, the press's performance has improved over the years. News personnel are better trained nowadays and less tolerant of practices that violate their professional code. Members of the Fourth Estate—all the concern over promotional ballyhoo and management of the news notwithstanding—are more than ever committed to a standard of objective reporting. Lapses do occur, but the nightmare, conjured up in novels such as George Orwell's *1984* and Eugene Burdick's *Sarkhan,* of a media-created reality—of fictitious wars in far-off lands manufactured to mold opinion at home—is remote as long as there is no political "1984." Competition among the news media still provides reasonable assurance against the manufacture of reality by prior agreement.

Nevertheless, the press is an institution, and, like most institutions, it reflects some point of view; it is, indeed, a natural extension of the societal Establishment. The financial holdings of the press are considerable, and its owners and managers have considerable status. Even though most reporters do not share this lofty prestige and position, they find a major reward in their work in the frequent contact they have with "important" people, people who are their chief sources of significant news. The importance of these informal networks for the flow of news can hardly be exaggerated; much of what goes on outside them remains unnoticed. In fact, the social character of news judgment is such that the status of a person helps determine whether his acts or experiences make "news." How else could one explain the failure of the news media in the United States to publicize adequately the conditions in Negro ghettos? Until large-scale protests and disturbances made headlines, the grievances of the segregated poor were not usually considered newsworthy.

Every communication system introduces its unique bias into the picture of reality it transmits. Some bias is inevitable. The image of events, as mirrored in the press, is always a little out of focus. Reporters working against deadlines cannot investigate every event. They will pay more attention to some than they merit; others they will underplay or totally ignore. At times a news story is not just a report *about* an event but *is* the event itself. The reporter who asks a question that can only provoke a denial may arouse suspicions that previously were without public significance. If the denial stirs a controversy, the reporter has created an event that becomes news. For instance, the "missile gap," which disappeared after the 1960 election, while not entirely a creation of the press, could not have become the crucial issue it did had it not so frequently been the subject of reporters' questions.

The media of mass communication, all together, create a "reality." Not all of reality, to be sure. But because mass communicators not only talk more to their audience than they listen but also listen more to one another than to their audience, there emerges a media-created focus of attention to which all who would participate in public life must orient themselves. Mass communication is predominantly one-way communication. There is, consequently, a lag in feedback that might correct any initial misperception or error in reporting events. In fact, public definitions of major events are essentially the upshot of all the efforts at every point to control—to exploit and facilitate as well as to impede—the flow of information to the public.

Most of what is known about public life reaches people secondhand. It does not involve direct observation. This holds for the television audience as much as for the audiences of the other news media. Hence, most people cannot know with total confidence that reports of remote events accurately convey what has taken place and what it means. They must take pretty much at face value what is reported. This is not to say that the public behaves like a herd of sheep, for it does indeed judge the news critically. But it lacks an adequate test for judging the validity of any item. Mainly, the members of a mass audience fall back on either one (or both) of two tests in evaluating the media content: the test of "affective congruence"—whether the report agrees with the individual's feelings and wishes—and the test of consistency—whether the report checks out with information from other sources. Affective congruence reinforces some misconceptions inasmuch as individuals tend to select their sources of information, giving more attention to reports that are congenial with their pre-existing point of view. The usefulness of the consistency test is also limited unless the various reports available represent independent observations. But they often do not—news personnel, who are generally heavy news consumers, check what they know against what other sources report; they often circulate and validate, in this way, any errors in the original account.

The Television Perspective

Does live television coverage provide a truer image of events, as many people suppose, or does it merely repeat and so reinforce any refraction introduced by the print media, by radio, or by newsreels? Our studies pointedly suggest that television, like other forms of mass communication, presents a refracted image of the events it reports. There is, however, one major difference: television journalists regard their technology as an ally in the quest for actuality, so much so that they sometimes defer to the camera to report the "facts," while denying responsibility if viewers misinterpret what is shown.

As we have seen, camera mobility is not enough to guarantee the faithful transmission of actuality, and the idea of letting the picture speak for itself enjoys far less acceptance than it did in the infant days of television. Some commentary is needed to link what is shown on camera to other developments that cannot be "seen" but nevertheless provide indispensable context for understanding the TV picture. Yet, the more television coverage depends on contextual information and explicit interpretation to tell a story, the more similar it becomes to newspaper reporting and the more open to the suspicion that, as in other media, the news it carries may be slanted.

When people claim that the camera "exposes the phony"—that by itself it can right a wrong impression —they have in mind its ability to catch public figures in some kind of sustained close-up so that detailed facial mien and bodily gestures are there for distant viewers to study. Does this guarantee that the viewer gets a more revealing picture of the person than he would otherwise have? Common sense answers "yes," but we have found that the opportunity to observe reactions in such detail can overshadow what is being said; the close-up highlights how the speaker looks as he is saying it. Does the radio listener, who lacks this vivid picture, pay more attention to what is being said? We need more controlled comparisons between the reactions of TV viewers and radio listeners than we now have. Some scanty evidence from the Kennedy-Nixon debates suggests that the dramatic improvement of Kennedy's personal image that followed the first debate did not extend to radio listeners. The relatively few who listened (mainly to car radios) were apt to call the debate a "draw," while viewers, who were witness to Kennedy's drive and energy and Nixon's apparent discomfort, credited Kennedy with a clear "win."

Nor can we be sure that a televised picture, such as that of two candidates locked in debate, is likely to "correct" previous misconceptions of their "real" character. Anxiety lest the close-up inadvertently reveal some trait best kept from public view exerts a restraining influence on television behavior. The same concern over his television personality likewise inhibits the give-and-take between the press and the man in office, whose behavior it is the function of the press to scrutinize. Those who compel public figures to submit voluntarily to sharp questioning by news panels, directly in front of the cameras, or to endure televised encounters (like the debates), tacitly invite and encourage the semi-fake, a form of publicity that puts a premium on stage management in a way that a radio transcription or the printed stenographic record does not.

The important point is that the televised event, however inauthentic and unrevealing, becomes the actuality. It is subsequently talked about, written about, and critically evaluated in newspapers, magazines, and other news media. Moreover, on some occasions, some news writers feel they can afford to defer to television for the coverage of spot news. In complex events like political conventions, in demonstrations like the 1963 March on Washington, major riots, and so forth, where the television coverage is itself major news, some reporters file dispatches based on the event viewed over TV. At other times, all the media pool their resources in one big operation, as in the reporting of the returns from the 1964 election. Thus media personnel pay more attention to the event as television reports it than to the event as it may have happened.

As we pointed out in connection with MacArthur Day, the television coverage injected a perspective of its own—but not one that disappointed prior expectations of what the event would be like, or one that transmitted a "true" picture of the event as experienced by spectators. The television image of events rather compounds the effects of whatever notions have already been made relevant by the press and prior broadcasts. With television news now a fact of life, the media will increasingly adjust their coverage to one another, each supplementing and, in part, repeating the coverage of the other. If television should come to take over the on-the-spot coverage of events—as it seems to be doing—time schedules and the need for equipment on the scene will invariably inject some refraction into the initial coverage of events.

If the mere presence of television—or any *public* scrutiny—causes some change in the behavior of a public figure, it also affects the way institutions function. "Acting for the camera" is perhaps a minor problem compared with the pervasive desire to accommodate to television. It affects even such time-honored institutions as the presidential press conference, which has ceased to be the occasion for an off-the-record briefing. No longer can a President frankly discuss certain problems, assured he will not be quoted as the "source." Any inadvertent remark before the camera and, especially, any request for its deletion before releasing the tape will surely become headline news. These are issues in which the impact of the media and of the event cannot be easily separated. The controversy over the influence of early returns on those who vote late has become relevant only because of the extensive use of electronic journalism.

The reciprocal effects of television on public life range from the minute and trivial to the deliberate staging of events. The whole pace and style of political campaigning adapts to the presence of television. For example, to avoid sensational but unanswerable charges on election morning, campaigns customarily ended before election eve. Now candidates vie for prime television time up to the time the polls open. Or, on election day itself, the candidates or their managers make public statements intended to offset in advance the effects they attribute to the rapid dissemination of returns by television. But the single most important reciprocal effect has been to make the "television personality" one of the important considerations in selecting a candidate for office.

The refraction inherent in the visual transmission of any complex event depends partly on how the technology is used. Unless TV newsmen are unusually self-searching, they only play back to the audience what has already been made familiar and acceptable by other media. The cameras will carry what the audience can most easily understand and spontaneously appreciate. Hence, the commitment of TV newsmen to the "picture worth a thousand words" does not suffice to communicate the significant "truth."

There is, of course, still another approach to objectivity. The camera can seek to juxtapose as much as possible a variety of opposing views. By employing commentators with divergent outlooks and by soliciting the views of spokesmen representing all possible opinion, the presentation offers the viewer a chance to choose among them. But this approach, too, has its own built-in sources of distortion. Finding "two sides" to every story—even where there is only "one"—sometimes creates an artificial picture of conflict. When TV publicizes deviant or irresponsible comments, it may only succeed in making them seem more important or popular than they are. Thus, leaders without a constituency have learned how to make use of television to appeal to the mass audience. So the attempt to be objective by giving unrestricted publicity probably exaggerates any reciprocal effect.

Electronic Participation

The technological capacity for instantaneous transmission of a picture is not an altogether unmixed blessing. The mobile camera opens new vistas on a world that now bears the imprint of television. But members of the audience may not be sufficiently mobile *psychologically* to keep up with the fast-changing scenes and characters conveyed by the camera. In connection with events during the 1952 conventions, we tried to show how complicated the job of the viewer was, and how great a challenge he faced in trying to understand what he was presumed to understand. To make sense of what he was shown of the proceedings, the viewer had to know something about the job of the chairman at the platform, know what a caucus was all about, what it was like to be a gallery spectator, a delegate, and so forth. However puzzled he might be by all that he saw, he was nevertheless reminded by commentators, again and again, that he was participating in the convention as a favored spectator, seeing all, glimpsing even what was hidden from many delegates.

The kind of coverage given to many public events amounts to an electronic transport to everywhere. The viewer becomes an "omniscient spectator." He is shown events from all available vantage points. We do not imply that viewers believe they actually see and know *everything* that is going on. But they do come to subscribe to the notion, constantly conveyed to them by the TV commentary and the press, that they "see for themselves," that they are directly involved in history, that television takes them to the scene of the crime, that they have a clearer picure of what is going on than people right "there." Whether viewers complain that commentators talk too much or talk too little, they believe themselves in either case to be less dependent upon reporters for the interpretation of what they can "see for themselves," so much indeed that they "know" when information is being kept from them.

The gist of the evidence is that people do not actually "see for themselves," but many still believe that they do. The effect of this belief may be as important as any effect of television that can be objectively documented. A belief in television as authentic experience makes it possible for viewers to validate their prejudices while increasing their self-confidence about their political expertise. They can assure this by not perceiving what they do not want to see, or by limiting their "participation" to what they understand. Viewers often lack the background to comprehend a good many of the events that "happen before their eyes." But no matter. They can decline to follow the camera and limit the number of personalities and the breadth of action they permit to reach their threshold of attention. In this way, they can overlook much of what goes on and fit the rest into available stereotypes.

Still, the unrestricted video coverage of complex events (like political conventions, campaigns, voting reports, and so forth), with their many shifts in focus, can promote a conception of these events as somehow manipulated. Believing that they "see for themselves," some viewers think that what they cannot understand is *evidence* that information is being withheld by politicians. For instance, when a network attempted to "let the viewer in on what was going on" at the 1952 nominating conventions by using a hidden camera (but no mike), this led some viewers to believe they were deliberately being kept out. One viewer, asked how he "knew" the convention had been "rigged," answered:

> I saw that caucus. They let us in on one state. I don't know which one now—South Carolina or Texas or one of those, I think. They wouldn't let the press in. It was down at the Hilton, led by the big bosses. You couldn't tell how the decisions were made. You couldn't hear anything. You could just see men standing around talking and saw just the backs of them.

Here is how another viewer "proved" that delegates were told how to vote by the bosses:

> Well, Michigan stood right up and said they had a caucus. That means that somebody was telling them what to do.

The point is that one can never take for granted that all or even most viewers will have enough experience and knowledge to discern all the available clues. Hence, many will continue to approach what is really specialized information through their own preconceptions, getting out of the televised events whatever meanings they are disposed to read into them. We think it very likely that an inverse relationship exists between the viewer's conviction about the validity of his own experience and his ability or willingness to learn from television. The more he believes he "sees for himself," the less he gains. If the video coverage of events is to contribute toward a better-informed public ready to exercise its franchise with a keen sense of discrimination, then the clarification of the factual and symbolic context of televised events demands as much, if not more, of the industry's attention as the quest for unrestricted publicity. The stress on "full coverage" strengthens the viewer's conviction that "seeing" is as good as "being there" and consequently makes it less likely that any false conclusions drawn from a telecast can be corrected by newspaper reports, commentator analysis, and so forth. More important, political telecasts that do not clarify "actuality" but have a special "ring of truth" may succeed in mobilizing emotions and indignation. This danger is inherent in the character of all mass media as one-way communication but probably more inherent in television.

The Cumulative Impact

Observations like those above point to the resiliency of preconceptions and prejudices. They have led to a "not uncommon tendency to go overboard in blindly minimizing the effects and potentialities of mass communications." [2] People do, to be sure, select from the political content transmitted by the media; they also

2. Klapper, *The Effects of Mass Communication*, p. 252.

interpret what they select, and they often reaffirm their beliefs by discussing what they hear or read with people whose outlook and background are similar to their own. But this is not the whole story. The media also structure a very real political environment which people can know about only through the media. Information about this environment is hard to escape. It filters through and affects even persons who are not directly exposed to the news or who deny that they are paying a great deal of attention to what the media say. There is something pervasive about the content of the mass media, something that can make its influence cumulative.

Most studies of the political effects of the mass media, including television, have concerned their influence on voting. They draw inferences about media effects mainly by studying individual voters' responses during periods of active political campaigning. But the purpose of the campaign is not so much to convert opinion as to reactivate and reinforce past loyalties. This, together with the basic stability in party allegiances, has made it difficult for the researcher to document the influence of the media on the voter. Can we conclude from such evidence that the influence of the mass media generally, and of television in particular, on voting behavior is minimal? We think not. On the contrary, the preconceptions and impressions that enter into a vote decision are gradually built up throughout the years between elections, and television plays a large part in shaping that political imagery. The studies in this book show how television, by its coverage of political events, both during and after electoral campaigns, influences viewers' impressions of political events and political personalities. Television, like radio and print, forces attention to some issues and ignores others, helps build up public images of political figures until they become familiar to all, and constantly suggests, by what is shown, the things individuals everywhere should know about, think about, have opinions about. The impressions so formed directly and indirectly, over the short and long run, affect voting behavior.

The way television handles the day-to-day flow of news by presenting a series of headline stories tends to highlight the unusual and extraordinary. Conflicts and crises predominate. Balanced presentation, that hallmark of good television reporting which gives equal time to charges and counter-charges, can, where contextual interpretation is inadequate, create a feeling that political events are beyond the scope of ordinary comprehension. Nor is the full coverage of an event enough to neutralize the inclinations of the chronically distrustful. It may only abet the tendency of viewers low in political competence to see in what they cannot understand proof that they are being manipulated.

Hence, television's style in chronicling political events can affect the fundamental orientation of the voter toward his government. It can undermine or bolster public confidence in the viability of political institutions and in the ability of political leaders to discharge their responsibilities. We are referring to something other than the public response to a specific decision or a specific news event—people constantly question the wisdom and motives of elected leaders in handling cold war issues, the racial crisis, economic discontent, and so forth. That is, after all, the mark of the informed citizen and the critical mind. Rather, we are referring to distrust of a more general and chronic nature, an attitude that only develops over time. This kind of distrust, which is of a distinctly projective nature, has its roots in the complexities of political life, complexities that lie beyond the understanding of all but the most politically sophisticated. The media, we contend, can stir up in individuals defensive reactions by their emphasis on crisis and conflict in lieu of clarifying normal decision-making processes.

Thus, the individual's resistance to appeals for political support is often rationalized by disgust about the low state of political ethics. Sometimes disgust may be fully justified, but often it is nothing but a defensive reaction against confusion, against reality that is overpowering, against the unfamiliar and the frightening, where "remote" events and invisible powers seem to determine the destiny of the individual who can do nothing about it. What about these "chronically distrustful" people? Do they distrust all news media, one as much as the other, and believe only what their friends tell them? Paradoxically, a generalized and exaggerated suspiciousness of politics and politicians often goes hand in hand with high reliance on some particular source of information, one these people somehow exempt from the contamination imputed to the mass media in their entirety. Since people must be able to form some credible picture about political questions, they seek the "truth" in some trusted source of information. Television often represents such a trusted source. It generally enjoys high credibility as a news medium among most of its viewers.

If TV tends to "personalize" politics, it is because it encourages viewers to scrutinize the motives of people who appear on the screen. These viewers focus less on what the *truth* is than on who can be *trusted*. Trusting in their own ability to know who can be trusted, they will accept policies they might otherwise oppose, so long as their advocate seems "sincere" and "honest." Even the most sophisticated viewer will lean on television for this kind of information during those periods when "whom to trust" seems more important than what any man stands for.

Undoubtedly, politics were personalized long before television arrived. The question is whether, since the advent of televised politics, elections have been, and are more likely to be, largely decided on the basis of "whom you trust more." In recent years much attention has been given in the press to public opinion polls that keep track of the "level of confidence" an officeholder enjoys. There has also been much talk about the "credibility gap." We have indicated some relationships between media usage and patterns of trust. Has any of this to do with television? Does high reliance on television go hand in hand with this emphasis on "trust" rather than on "truth"? In a number of recent elections, there has been widespread ticket-splitting. Is this a phenomenon traceable to the intimate view television is believed to afford? Or a response to the stage-managed personality? Or does ticket-splitting merely reflect the growing sophistication of the American electorate and have nothing to do with television and the way it is used?

What about the influence of television on the mood of the public? Writing in the *New York Times* in August, 1967, when the United States was vexed with war in Vietnam and riots in the large cities, James Reston, traveling around the United States, wrote that "there was an uneasy feeling that things were going wrong in the cities and abroad, but that the people couldn't help it, and didn't quite understand it, and therefore had to tolerate it, even if they didn't like it, because they had no present alternative to it." Television makes it possible for people to be on the battlefield at Vietnam and the battlefield at Detroit; yet they cannot really do anything about Vietnam and Detroit. They form opinions, as Reston points out, but seem to think their opinions amount to nothing. Is this merely a mood of the moment or is it, at least in part, the inevitable consequence of the unique and overwhelming view of the world—so near and yet so far and so unfathomable—that has come our way through television every day?

No one has yet been able to "demonstrate" through a convincing experiment what the long-range effects of television have been. Nor are they likely to. To trace a change in a political climate or a realignment within the electorate straight to the door of television is a task foredoomed to failure. Yet, failure to "prove" the cumulative effects does not mean that political life has been unaffected or, for that matter, that small incremental changes (such as the improvement in Kennedy's image) may not be cumulative in their effect.

We have tried to find some clues to these cumulative effects by looking at the way television transmits reality and affects the imagery of politics and political figures. If television has been transforming the nature of political life, it is in the images it transmits that we have to find the answers.

INDEX

QUADRANGLE PAPERBACKS

American History

Frederick Lewis Allen. *The Lords of Creation.* (QP35)
Lewis Atherton. *Main Street on the Middle Border.* (QP36)
Thomas A. Bailey. *Woodrow Wilson and the Lost Peace.* (QP1)
Thomas A. Bailey. *Woodrow Wilson and the Great Betrayal.* (QP2)
Charles A. Beard. *The Idea of National Interest.* (QP27)
Carl L. Becker. *Everyman His Own Historian.* (QP33)
Barton J. Bernstein. *Politics and Policies of the Truman Administration.* (QP72)
Ray A. Billington. *The Protestant Crusade.* (QP12)
Allan G. Bogue. *From Prairie to Corn Belt.* (QP50)
Kenneth E. Boulding. *The Organizational Revolution.* (QP43)
Robert V. Bruce. *1877: Year of Violence.* (QP73)
Gerald M. Capers. *John C. Calhoun, Opportunist.* (QP70)
David M. Chalmers. *Hooded Americanism.* (QP51)
John Chamberlain. *Farewell to Reform.* (QP19)
Alice Hamilton Cromie. *A Tour Guide to the Civil War.*
Robert D. Cross. *The Emergence of Liberal Catholicism in America.* (QP44)
Richard M. Dalfiume. *American Politics Since 1945.* (NYTimes Book, QP57)
Carl N. Degler. *The New Deal.* (NYTimes Book, QP74)
Chester McArthur Destler. *American Radicalism, 1865-1901.* (QP30)
Robert A. Divine. *American Foreign Policy Since 1945.* (NYTimes Book, QP58)
Robert A. Divine. *Causes and Consequences of World War II.* (QP63)
Robert A. Divine. *The Illusion of Neutrality.* (QP45)
Elisha P. Douglass. *Rebels and Democrats.* (QP26)
Felix Frankfurter. *The Commerce Clause.* (QP16)
Lloyd C. Gardner. *A Different Frontier.* (QP32)
Edwin Scott Gaustad. *The Great Awakening in New England.* (QP46)
Ray Ginger. *Altgeld's America.* (QP21)
Ray Ginger. *Modern American Cities.* (NYTimes Book, QP67)
Ray Ginger. *Six Days or Forever?* (QP68)
Gerald N. Grob. *Workers and Utopia.* (QP61)
Louis Hartz. *Economic Policy and Democratic Thought.* (QP52)
William B. Hesseltine. *Lincoln's Plan of Reconstruction.* (QP41)
Granville Hicks. *The Great Tradition.* (QP62)
Dwight W. Hoover. *Understanding Negro History.* (QP49)
Stanley P. Hirshson. *Farewell to the Bloody Shirt.* (QP53)
Frederic C. Howe. *The Confessions of a Reformer.* (QP39)
Harold L. Ickes. *The Autobiography of a Curmudgeon.* (QP69)
Louis Joughin and Edmund M. Morgan. *The Legacy of Sacco and Vanzetti.* (QP7)
William Loren Katz. *Teachers' Guide to American Negro History.* (QP210)
Burton Ira Kaufman. *Washington's Farewell Address.* (QP64)
Edward Chase Kirkland. *Dream and Thought in the Business Community, 1860-1900.* (QP11)
Edward Chase Kirkland. *Industry Comes of Age.* (QP42)
Adrienne Koch. *The Philosophy of Thomas Jefferson.* (QP17)
Gabriel Kolko. *The Triumph of Conservatism.* (QP40)
Walter LaFeber. *John Quincy Adams and American Continental Empire.* (QP23)
Lawrence H. Leder. *The Meaning of the American Revolution.* (NYTimes Book, QP66)
David E. Lilienthal. *TVA: Democracy on the March.* (QP28)
Arthur S. Link. *Wilson the Diplomatist.* (QP18)
Huey P. Long. *Every Man a King.* (QP8)
Gene M. Lyons. *America: Purpose and Power.* (QP24)
Jackson Turner Main. *The Antifederalists.* (QP14)
Ernest R. May. *The World War and American Isolation, 1914-1917.* (QP29)
Henry F. May. *The End of American Innocence.* (QP9)
Thomas J. McCormick. *China Market.* (QP75)
George E. Mowry. *The California Progressives.* (QP6)
William L. O'Neill. *American Society Since 1945.* (NYTimes Book, QP59)
Frank L. Owsley. *Plain Folk of the Old South.* (QP22)
David Graham Phillips. *The Treason of the Senate.* (QP20)
Julius W. Pratt. *Expansionists of 1898.* (QP15)
C. Herman Pritchett. *The Roosevelt Court.* (QP71)
Moses Rischin. *The American Gospel of Success.* (QP54)
John P. Roche. *The Quest for the Dream.* (QP47)
David A. Shannon. *The Socialist Party of America.* (QP38)
Andrew Sinclair. *The Available Man.* (QP60)

American History (continued)

John Spargo. *The Bitter Cry of the Children.* (QP55)
Bernard Sternsher. *The Negro in Depression and War.* (QP65)
Richard W. Van Alstyne. *The Rising American Empire.* (QP25)
Willard M. Wallace. *Appeal to Arms.* (QP10)
Norman Ware. *The Industrial Worker, 1840-1860.* (QP13)
Albert K. Weinberg. *Manifest Destiny.* (QP3)
Bernard A. Weisberger. *They Gathered at the River.* (QP37)
Robert H. Wiebe. *Businessmen and Reform.* (QP56)
William Appleman Williams. *The Contours of American History.* (QP34)
William Appleman Williams. *The Great Evasion.* (QP48)
Esmond Wright. *Causes and Consequences of the American Revolution.* (QP31)

European History

William Sheridan Allen. *The Nazi Seizure of Power.* (QP302)
W. O. Henderson. *The Industrial Revolution in Europe.* (QP303)
Raul Hilberg. *The Destruction of the European Jews.* (QP301)
Richard N. Hunt. *German Social Democracy.* (QP306)
Telford Taylor. *Sword and Swastika.* (QP304)
John Weiss. *Nazis and Fascists in Europe, 1918-1945.* (NYTimes Book, QP305)

Philosophy

F. H. Bradley. *The Presuppositions of Critical History.* (QP108)
William Earle. *Objectivity.* (QP109)
James M. Edie, James P. Scanlan, Mary-Barbara Zeldin, George L. Kline. *Russian Philosophy.* (3 vols, QP111, 112, 113)
James M. Edie. *An Invitation to Phenomenology.* (QP103)
James M. Edie. *New Essays in Phenomenology.* (QP114)
James M. Edie. *Phenomenology in America.* (QP105)
R. O. Elveton. *The Phenomenology of Husserl.* (QP116)
Manfred S. Frings. *Heidegger and the Quest for Truth.* (QP107)
Moltke S. Gram. *Kant: Disputed Questions.* (QP104)
James F. Harris, Jr., and Richard Severens. *Analyticity.* (QP117)
E. D. Klemke. *Studies in the Philosophy of G. E. Moore.* (QP115)
Lionel Rubinoff. *Faith and Reason.* (QP106)
Stuart F. Spicker. *The Philosophy of the Body.* (QP118)
Paul Tibbetts. *Perception.* (QP110)
Pierre Thévenaz. *What Is Phenomenology?* (QP101)

Social Science

Shalom Endleman. *Violence in the Streets.* (QP215)
Nathan Glazer. *Cities in Trouble.* (NYTimes Book, QP212)
George and Eunice Grier. *Equality and Beyond.* (QP204)
Kurt Lang and Gladys Engel Lang. *Politics and Television.* (QP216)
Charles O. Lerche, Jr. *Last Chance in Europe.* (QP207)
Raymond W. Mack. *Prejudice and Race Relations.* (NYTimes Book, QP217)
David Mitrany. *A Working Peace System.* (QP205)
H. L. Nieburg. *In the Name of Science.* (QP218)
Martin Oppenheimer. *The Urban Guerrilla.* (QP219)
Martin Oppenheimer and George Lakey. *A Manual for Direct Action.* (QP202)
James Parkes. *Antisemitism.* (QP213)
Fred Powledge. *To Change a Child.* (QP209)
Lee Rainwater. *And the Poor Get Children.* (QP208)
The Rockefeller Report on the Americas. (QP214)
Clarence Senior. *The Puerto Ricans.* (QP201)
Harold L. Sheppard. *Poverty and Wealth in America.* (NYTimes Book, QP220)
Arthur L. Stinchcombe. *Rebellion in a High School.* (QP211)
Harry M. Trebing. *The Corporation in the American Economy.* (NYTimes Book, QP221)
David Manning White. *Pop Culture in America.* (NYTimes Book, QP222)